GOURMET IRELAND

GOURMET IRELAND

Paul and Jeanne Rankin

BBC BOOKS

NOTE FOR VEGETARIANS

Recipes suitable for vegetarians
are marked with a (**V**) symbol.
Please note that these may include
cheese and other dairy products.

This book is published to accompany the
television series entitled *Gourmet Ireland*
which was first broadcast in 1994

Published by BBC Books,
an imprint of BBC Worldwide Publishing.
BBC Worldwide Limited, Woodlands,
80 Wood Lane, London W12 0TT

First published 1994
Reprinted 1994 (twice)

First published in paperback 1995

© Paul and Jeanne Rankin 1994
The moral rights of the authors have been asserted

ISBN 0 563 37155 2

Designed by Bill Mason
Photographs by Graham Kirk
Styling by Helen Payne

Set in Berkeley Old Style by Selwood Systems, Midsomer Norton
Printed and bound in Great Britain by Butler & Tanner Ltd, Frome
Colour separation by Radstock Reproductions, Midsomer Norton
Cover printed by Clays Ltd, St Ives plc

Contents

ABOUT THE AUTHORS

Paul Rankin, from County Down in Northern Ireland, and Jeanne, from Winnipeg in Canada, met whilst working on a boat in Greece when they were both twenty and travelling the world. To finance their travels they worked as waiters and in restaurant kitchens, but cooking soon became their passion. On the advice of a French chef in Australia, they went to London for professional training and were taken on by Albert Roux, Paul at *Le Gavroche* and Jeanne at *Le Poulbort* and *Gavvers*. In 1984 they married and in 1986, with their first child, they moved to Canada. A year later Paul took charge of a kitchen in a hotel in northern California. Here, for the first time, he was able to develop his own ideas for recipes and presentation.

The Rankins came back to Ireland in 1989 with their two daughters, bought a bankrupt Belfast restaurant and *Roscoff* was born. In a city where there was a shortage of outstanding restaurants it soon made its name and has gone from strength to strength, while the Rankins have become well known as two of the most creative and popular chefs working in the United Kingdom today.

ACKNOWLEDGMENTS

We take this opportunity to thank Brian Waddell, producer of the *Gourmet Ireland* TV series. Without his inspiration it might never have been. We would also like to thank Maria McCann, the assistant producer, and all the film crew.

We owe a great deal to the wonderful growers, producers and suppliers, whom we met when making the television series, for their knowledge and time, their devotion and energy. We truly thank all of them, too numerous to list here.

Our gratitude extends to John and Sally McKenna, whose research and knowledge helped so much to develop the Irish food scene.

Finally, and most important of all, the staff at Roscoff, our restaurant in Belfast, deserve our heartfelt thanks, for their hard work and support over the years.

INTRODUCTION

Gourmet Ireland: to many people these two words seem a contradiction in terms. In their minds, food in this country conjures up heaps of overcooked meat piled up on a plate with underseasoned boiled root vegetables alongside – nothing 'gourmet' about it. But Irish cooking and Irish food do not necessarily mean the same thing.

When we were first asked to suggest a concept for a cookery programme, it was the food products of this island that we got really excited about. Here was something that we felt more people had to know about. We ourselves were typical examples of those who wrongly stereotyped images of Irish food. In 1989 we returned to Belfast from the Napa valley in California. Out there, a chef is swamped with choice; everything is available, nothing is a problem. As we worked feverishly at getting Roscoff's doors open, we worried that we would not be able to obtain products that would be of a good enough quality. After all, we had just come from one of the food world's most exciting and progressive hot spots. Could a small island like Ireland ever measure up to such a developed hub?

To say that we were in for a pleasant surprise is an understatement; we still, nearly five years on, marvel at the true state of affairs. The more we look, the more we find. There is an absolute goldmine of products, and hand in hand a wealth of people working to develop and supply them. It is these growers, producers and suppliers that should be encouraged and supported, and we decided that, in our tv series and our book, we had the opportunity to do just that.

To film the series we travelled all over Ireland, from the green glens of Antrim in the north to the rich pasturelands of County Cork in the south, to the fishing ports along the coasts and to the colourful markets of inland towns up and down the country, talking and tasting, seeing and learning. We wanted to discover just what was being done on this little island in the name of food. We found that things in Ireland are really on the move. The people in the industry – be they the farmer, cheesemaker, fisherman, or market-man – are really committed to excellence. They recognize the benefits of the climate and the countryside untouched by industrialization, and they see that Irish produce has unrivalled natural goodness and variety.

In this book, as well as highlighting Ireland's tremendous products, we have created a variety of recipes which emphasize our tastes and background. There are a few of our favourite Irish dishes, but the majority are simply modern, exciting dishes that reflect our training in London and North America, and our travels throughout Asia, India and China. Our experiences led us towards honest food, simple and pure flavours, letting the ingredients speak out. Regardless of what country, or cuisine it was, the best meals, the lingering memories, all had one common thread, and that was the quality of the ingredients.

Our trip around Ireland, and the many interesting characters whom we met, will remain with us the rest of our lives.

P&JR

CHAPTER

1

THE CHEESE-MAKER

O NE WOULD IMAGINE that with such a wealth of lush, pure pastures, Ireland would also have a great tradition of cheese-making. In actual fact, although there has always been a wee bit about, it is really only in the last fifteen years that the cheese-makers have come into their own. From barely a dozen in production in the early 1980s, one can now choose from over 170 varieties. Can any other product boast of such a fantastic revival?

'Why has it happened?' one might logically ask. The renaissance of the cottage industry scene in general has probably been one of the biggest factors. More and more Europeans have settled in Ireland in the last decade, opting for a quieter country lifestyle which they can no longer find in their homelands (compared to parts of Europe, Ireland is still underdeveloped and underpopulated). These immigrants bring with them their crafts as well as their tastes. As people travel abroad more they return with more liberated ideas towards different foods, different tastes. They've learned that there's more to cheese than Cheddar. And of course, the tourist industry is always there, loving all things made in Ireland.

Flavour and variety begins with the type of milk: cows', sheep's or goats'. It can also be influenced by the animals' diet: green meadows, wild flowers, sparse heather and gorse, and so on. Really though, from the separating of the curds, the options are dealt by the cheese-maker: how he cuts the curd, how he salts it, how he moulds and, of course, how and where he matures his cheeses. It is wonderful to be so spoilt by such an array of types, tastes and textures!

A great number of these Irish cheeses, far too numerous to list, have attained international recognition and with CAIS, the Irish Farmhouse Cheese-makers Guild, representing and helping to promote them, the adventurous cheese-maker can only go in one direction – forward.

Just remember that transportation, packaging and storage can all be damaging to cheese if it's not treated properly throughout these stages, so if you can, try to buy direct. If not – and this is just about as good – find a dependable supplier. You'll be missing out if you don't.

BAKED CHEDDAR AND SCALLION SOUP

A HOMESPUN VERSION OF THE CLASSIC FRENCH ONION SOUP, DO TRY THIS AS IT'S JUST AS GOOD. IF YOU DECIDE TO BLEND THE SOUP BASE IT MAKES IT MUCH EASIER: YOU DON'T HAVE TO SLICE THE ONIONS SO FINELY AND YOU DON'T HAVE TO MAKE THE ROUX SEPARATELY.

SERVES 4–6

700g (1½lb) onions, sliced

4 tablespoons unsalted butter

350ml (12 fl oz) dry white wine

3 tablespoons flour

2 litres (3½ pints) vegetable or chicken stock

1 bouquet garni

salt and freshly ground white pepper

1 egg yolk

100ml (3½ fl oz) single cream

300g (11oz) Cheddar, grated

1 bunch spring onions, thinly sliced

8–12 slices stale baguette, toasted

Pre-heat the oven to Gas Mark 6/200°C/400°F.

Sweat the onions in half the butter without letting them colour. Add the wine and continue to cook until the wine has almost evaporated.

Meanwhile, make a light *roux* by melting the remaining butter in a small pan. Add the flour and cook gently without colouring for 2 minutes, stirring. Allow the *roux* to cool slightly then whisk the stock on to the *roux* until you have a smooth, lightly thickened stock. Add this to the onions with the bouquet garni and a little salt. Simmer gently for about 30 minutes. Taste carefully and season with salt and ground white pepper.

At this stage, you may blend the soup in a food processor to make it smooth and thick, or leave it with the onion slices whole.

To serve, blend together the egg yolk and cream and add 2 tablespoons of this liaison to each ovenproof bowl and sprinkle half the cheese and spring onions on top. Pour the hot soup over this and add 2 slices of baguette. Top with the remaining spring onions and cheese. Bake in the pre-heated oven for at least 5 minutes until the top is bubbling and crusty brown.

PEPPERY PIZZAS WITH ARDRAHAN CHEESE

EVERYONE LOVES PIZZA AND THIS IS A PERSONAL FAVOURITE. NICE AND SPICY, FRESH AND NATURAL, IT'S JUST THE TICKET. USE ANY FAVOURITE CHEESE, THOUGH NOT THE FAKE PROCESSED STUFF. ARDRAHAN CHEESE COMES FROM COUNTY CORK AND IS MADE FROM PASTEURIZED COWS' MILK. IT IS SIMILAR TO DANISH HAVARTI.

MAKES 6 INDIVIDUAL PIZZAS

FOR THE BASES

6 Gourmet Pizza Bases (see p. 179)

FOR THE SAUCE

1 small onion, finely chopped

1 garlic clove

2 tablespoons olive oil

2 red peppers, seeded and sliced

3 ripe tomatoes, skinned, seeded and roughly chopped

1 tablespoon tomato purée

salt and freshly ground black pepper

FOR THE TOPPINGS

450g (1lb) oyster mushrooms or button mushrooms

4 tablespoons olive oil

3 chilli peppers, mild or hot as preferred, seeded and sliced

2 red onions, sliced

1 bunch of fresh coriander

450g (1lb) favourite cheese

Pre-heat the oven to Gas Mark 6/200°C/400°F.

To make the sauce, sweat the onion and garlic in the oil over a medium heat until they are soft and transparent. Add the peppers, tomatoes and tomato purée. Cover and cook over a medium-low heat for about 20 minutes. Season with salt and pepper.

To prepare the toppings, trim the oyster or button mushrooms and fry over a high heat in 1 tablespoon of olive oil until soft. Season with salt and pepper and set aside.

Fry the chilli peppers gently in 1 tablespoon of olive oil until soft. Season with salt and pepper and set aside.

Fry the onions in the remaining oil until soft but not browned. Set aside.

Pick the coriander leaves off the bunch and chop them roughly. Set aside. Slice the cheese into fairly thin slices; too thick and it won't melt properly.

Spread some of the sauce on to each pizza base (which will be cooled or nearly so). Divide the toppings evenly over the 6 bases and bake in the pre-heated oven for about 5 minutes until the cheese is melted and bubbly and starting to brown. Serve at once.

OVERLEAF

Left: *Baked Goats' Cheese with Roast Beetroot* (page 16)

Right: *Lemon-scented Cheese and Berry Tartlette* (page 20)

BAKED GOATS' CHEESE WITH ROAST BEETROOT

(V)

SOME MARRIAGES SEEM MADE IN HEAVEN AND THIS ONE CERTAINLY IS.
EACH FLAVOUR IS STRONG ENOUGH TO BALANCE THE OTHER YET STILL REMAINS DISTINCT.
THE DISH HAS NICE TEXTURE CONTRASTS, TOO.

SERVES 4

450g (1lb) baby beetroots

450g (1lb) goats' cheese

1 tablespoon walnut oil

60g (2½oz) coarse home-made breadcrumbs

a few mixed salad leaves such as rocket, frisée or cos

60g (2½oz) walnuts, roasted and skinned

FOR THE WALNUT VINAIGRETTE

1 teaspoon Dijon mustard

salt and freshly ground black pepper

2 teaspoons white wine vinegar

50ml (2 fl oz) peanut oil

50ml (2 fl oz) walnut oil

To prepare the vinaigrette, dissolve the mustard and a dash of salt and pepper in the wine vinegar. Whisk or stir in the oils. Taste for seasoning and adjust the salt and pepper if necessary.

Pre-heat the oven to Gas Mark 3/160°C/325°F.

Wash and trim each bulb of beetroot. Wrap them individually in kitchen foil and cook in the pre-heated oven for about 1 hour until tender. Remove from the oven and allow to cool. Peel carefully. Cut into 5mm (¼in) thick slices and marinate these in some of the vinaigrette.

Increase the oven temperature to Gas Mark 5/190°C/375°F.

Peel the goat cheese of any rind and slice into 2cm (¾in) thick rounds. Brush with some walnut oil then coat evenly with the breadcrumbs. Bake in the pre-heated oven for about 10 minutes until the cheese is heated through and melting at the edges.

Dress the salad leaves with the walnut vinaigrette and arrange in the centre of 4 plates. Place the toasted goats' cheese on top. Arrange several slices of beetroot around the salad and drizzle with a little of the vinaigrette. Garnish with the roast walnuts, sprinkling around and over the salad and beetroot.

WILTED CABBAGE SALAD WITH BACON AND CASHEL BLUE CHEESE

A WARM, WINTERY SALAD WITH SAVOURY FLAVOURS THAT ENTICE AND WIN OVER EVEN THOSE WHO THINK THEY DON'T LIKE CABBAGE. YOU CAN USE ANY FAVOURITE BLUE CHEESE – SUCH AS STILTON OR ROQUEFORT – FOR THIS RECIPE.

SERVES 6

3 slices white bread, cut into 1cm ($\frac{1}{2}$in) cubes

6 tablespoons duck or goose fat

200g (7oz) streaky bacon, cut into 5cm (2in) pieces

1 garlic clove, chopped

3 tablespoons red wine vinegar

salt and freshly ground black pepper

1 Savoy cabbage, thick ribs removed and leaves sliced

$\frac{1}{2}$ head of radicchio, thinly sliced

200g (7oz) Cashel or other blue cheese, crumbled

Pre-heat the oven to Gas Mark 4/180°C/350°F.

To make the croûtons, toss the bread cubes in 2 tablespoons of duck or goose fat and bake in the pre-heated oven for about 10 minutes, tossing and turning frequently until they are golden brown and crusty.

To make the dressing, sauté the bacon pieces in 2 tablespoons of duck or goose fat in a large frying-pan over moderate heat until the bacon is beginning to crisp nicely. Remove the bacon with a slotted spoon, add the garlic and let it fry gently for 1 minute.

Remove from the heat and carefully add the wine vinegar. Scrape the bottom of the pan to loosen any caramelized juices. Taste the hot dressing for salt and add some freshly ground black pepper.

To wilt the cabbage, heat a very large frying-pan with the remaining duck or goose fat over a moderate heat. Add the cabbage all at once. Cook, stirring, for about 1½ minutes until the cabbage has wilted. Tip into a large bowl.

To serve, combine the radicchio, bacon, cheese and croûtons with the warm cabbage and toss with the dressing of red wine and juices. Spoon some of the mixture into a 10cm (4in) biscuit cutter or cooking ring and press down slightly until the cabbage mixture forms a neat shape. Carefully remove the ring. Repeat with all the cabbage and arrange the cabbage rings on warmed plates. Serve at once.

DARK CHOCOLATE CHEESECAKE WITH RASPBERRY COULIS

EVERYONE SHOULD HAVE A GOOD CHEESECAKE RECIPE. IT KEEPS WELL, CAN BE MADE A COUPLE OF
DAYS IN ADVANCE AND IS ALWAYS A REAL CROWD PLEASER! THE QUANTITIES GIVEN
HERE WILL MAKE ABOUT 400G (14OZ) OF PRALINE. YOU CAN STORE THE EXTRA IN AN AIRTIGHT
CONTAINER FOR A MONTH OR SO. IT IS WONDERFUL SPRINKLED OVER ICE-CREAM OR BISCUITS.
WE USUALLY USE A FOOD PROCESSOR FOR THIS RECIPE.

SERVES 10–12

FOR THE PRALINE

300g (11oz) whole hazelnuts

100g (4oz) sugar

4 tablespoons water

FOR THE BASE

150g (5oz) hazelnut praline

*300g (11oz) digestive biscuits
(or half rich tea and half
digestive)*

*50g (2oz) unsalted butter,
melted*

FOR THE FILLING

*1kg (2¼lb) full-fat soft cheese,
at room temperature*

4 eggs

*200ml (7fl oz) crème fraîche
or soured cream*

*500g (1lb 2oz) plain
chocolate, melted and cooled*

1 tablespoon vanilla essence

*50ml (2fl oz) cognac or rum
(optional)*

FOR THE COULIS

225g (8oz) raspberries

*200ml (7fl oz) Sugar Syrup
(see p. 188)*

juice of 1 lemon

Pre-heat the oven to Gas Mark 4/180°C/350°F. Grease a baking tray.

To make the praline, place the hazelnuts on a baking tray and toast in the pre-heated oven for about 10 minutes until skins are dark but not black. Remove skins by either rubbing nuts together in a tea towel or in a wire mesh basket such as one from a deep-fryer. Nearly all the skins should be removed and the hazelnuts should be a golden brown.

Place the sugar and water in a heavy-based pan and stir over a low heat until the sugar has dissolved. Continue to cook over a high heat, brushing down the sides of the pan as the sugar cooks to avoid crystallization. This can be done with a pastry brush dipped in water. When the caramel is medium brown it is ready.

Place the hazelnuts on the

prepared baking tray. Pour the caramel carefully over the nuts, trying to coat all of them. Use a spatula to fold the caramel and nuts over to ensure the caramel is evenly distributed. Leave to cool. Break into smallish pieces then crush or pulse in a food processor until coarsely ground.

Reduce the oven temperature to Gas Mark 3/160°C/ 325°F. Grease a 23–25cm (9–10in) spring-release cake tin.

To make the base, weigh out the praline and crush or process in a food processor until medium fine. Pour into a bowl. Crush or process the biscuits in a food processor until very fine then add to the praline. Pour in the melted butter and mix the ingredients together. The mixture

should be fairly sticky but not wet.

Press into the prepared cake tin so that the mixture covers the base to a depth of about 5mm ($\frac{1}{4}$in). You may not need to use all the mixture.

To make the filling, beat the cheese until smooth. Add the eggs and mix until just combined. Add the *crème fraîche* or soured cream, chocolate, vanilla essence and cognac or rum, if using, and mix until combined, wiping down the sides once or twice if you are using a processor to ensure there are no lumps. Gently pour into the cake tin and bake for about 1–1$\frac{1}{4}$ hours or until the whole top of the cheesecake looks set and does not wobble.

To make the raspberry coulis, place the raspberries, sugar syrup and lemon juice in a blender and process until well blended. Rub through a fine mesh sieve to remove all the seeds. Taste and if necessary adjust by adding either a little more sugar syrup or lemon juice. This sauce can be frozen or kept in the fridge for several days.

To serve, slice the set cheesecake using a knife which has been dipped into hot water and quickly dried to give a smooth cut. Carefully, with a palette knife, place the pieces on to chilled plates and surround them with the raspberry sauce. If desired, the cheesecake can be topped with a sprinkling of hazelnut praline.

LEMON-SCENTED CHEESE AND BERRY TARTLETTES

THE LIGHT LEMON CHEESE MIXTURE IS CREAMY AND TANGY AND IS A PERFECT BALANCE FOR SWEET BERRIES. CHOOSE RIPE, UNBRUISED BERRIES, WHATEVER IS IN SEASON WILL ALWAYS TASTE BEST.

SERVES 4

250g (9oz) Sweet Shortcrust Pastry (see p. 184)

1 egg yolk, lightly beaten

400g (14oz) berries (raspberries, blackberries, strawberries, currants, etc.)

FOR THE FILLING

225g (8oz) full-fat soft cheese

150ml (5 fl oz) soured cream

1 egg

75g (3oz) caster sugar

¾ teaspoon vanilla essence

finely grated rind and juice of ½ lemon

icing sugar for sprinkling

Pre-heat the oven to Gas Mark 4/180°C/350°F. Lightly grease 4 × 10cm (4in) tartlette moulds.

To prepare tartlette shells, roll the sweet shortcrust out to just 3mm (⅛in) thickness and use to line the prepared moulds. Place in the fridge to chill for at least 20 minutes.

Cover the pastry with greaseproof paper, fill with baking beans and bake blind in the pre-heated oven for about 10 minutes until golden brown. Remove the paper and beans and brush the insides lightly with egg yolk. Set aside to cool.

Reduce oven temperature to Gas Mark 2/150°C/300°F.

To prepare the filling, Whisk all the filling ingredients together either in a mixer or by hand until smooth and homogenous. Taste for flavour. Depending on the lemon, you may want to add slightly more lemon juice or slightly more sugar. You do want the filling to be nice and tart to balance the natural sweetness of the berries.

Spoon the filling into the pre-baked tartlette moulds, taking care not to spill any over the edges of the pastry, and place in the pre-heated oven to bake for just 8 minutes. The filling should still be wobbly in the centre when you remove them from the oven. (Remember, it will continue to cook even after being removed from the oven). Leave to cool.

When the tartlettes are cool, remove them from the moulds. Carefully heap a pile of the chosen berries in a generous fashion on top of the fillings. A sprinkling of icing sugar over the berries adds an attractive finish to the tartlettes. This can be served with either a dollop of whipped cream, or Raspberry Coulis (see p. 18) or both.

CHAPTER

2

THE SMOKERY

SMOKING HAS ALWAYS been a traditional method of food preservation. Here in Ireland, there is a great history of smoke-houses and there is still a great demand for the finished products. Meat, poultry and fish would first be salted, either by dry salting or by being immersed in a salty solution called a brine. The length of time the product is cured in this way varies greatly, but generally there is a trend for a lighter hand these days, now that it is more of a sought-after flavour as opposed to a vital preserving technique. This curing and the length of time of the actual smoking both contribute greatly to the flavour and texture of the finished product.

Fish must be the most commonly smoked food in Ireland. Indeed, her best known speciality food is smoked salmon. Appreciated as a gourmet product throughout North America, Europe and Scandinavia, its exquisite flavour and melting texture raise it on to a well deserved pedestal. However, do not underestimate some of the other fish that lend themselves to smoking. Smoked eel, thoroughly undervalued in Britain and Ireland, is considered a gourmet's delight in Europe. Then there is haddock, cod, trout and, of course, who hasn't heard of kippers, a type of smoked herring.

Nowadays, smoked chicken and pheasant are becoming very popular as are smoked beef, pork and more recently, cheese.

Traditionally, oak is the favourite wood to use in the smoke-house, but other hardwoods, such as hickory, maple and cherrywood, are all due to come into their own. Obviously, each imparts a different flavour to the product. Every smoke-house has its own personal favourite just as each has its own exacting formula. Some claim the secret is in the brine, others, the type of wood and still more, the length of smoking time or a combination of these factors.

To our minds, the most important criterion is to start with a good, fresh product. An inferior one will only be masked, not improved upon, by the techniques involved. Thankfully, the use of dyes as a method of lending colour to the product is fast becoming unpopular and is dying out. We would doubt anything that turned our fingers yellow or orange as we worked with it.

Smoked foods can be eaten at any stage of a meal. There are no hard and fast rules to stick to, just follow your own taste buds.

CELERIAC SOUP WITH SMOKED PHEASANT

THIS IS A WONDERFUL HEARTY SOUP THAT IS SIMPLE YET SOUNDS QUITE GLAMOROUS.
IF YOU CAN'T FIND SMOKED PHEASANT, USE SOME SMOKED HAM, OR EVEN BACON.

SERVES 6–8

50g (2oz) unsalted butter

2 medium onions, peeled and sliced

1 bulb of celeriac, peeled and cut into 2cm ($\frac{3}{4}$ in) dice

1 smoked pheasant carcass, plus drumsticks

1 bay leaf

2 litres ($3\frac{1}{2}$ pints) water

salt and freshly ground white pepper

4 tablespoons whipping cream, lightly whipped (optional)

2 tablespoons chopped parsley

In a large pot, melt the butter over a medium heat and sweat the onions for about 10 minutes, until they are just starting to colour. Add the celeriac, the smoked pheasant, bay leaf, water and salt. Bring to the boil, and skim off any scum which rises to the surface. Turn the heat down to low, and simmer gently for 30 minutes.

Remove from the heat, take out the carcass, the drumsticks, and the bay leaf. After the carcass has cooled, pry off small pieces of meat. Take all the meat off the drumsticks as well, chop roughly, and reserve.

Purée the soup in a blender to a nice smooth consistency, and adjust the seasoning adding salt and pepper as necessary.

Place a little of the pheasant meat in the bottom of each warmed soup bowl and ladle in the soup on top. Garnish with a swirl of the lightly whipped cream and with a sprinkle of chopped parsley.

SMOKED PHEASANT SALAD WITH CREAMED LENTILS AND ROAST GARLIC

SMOKED POULTRY IS AN EXCELLENT AND VERSATILE PRODUCT. TRY THIS SALAD WITH SMOKED CHICKEN, DUCK OR TURKEY. KEEP ANY BONES FOR STOCK AND USE THAT FOR YOUR NEXT BATCH OF CELERY OR LENTIL SOUP.

SERVES 4

120g (4½oz) green lentils

600ml (1 pint water)

2 tablespoons chopped carrot

2 tablespoons chopped leek

2 tablespoons chopped onion

1 sprig of fresh parsley

1½ teaspoons dried thyme

1 garlic bulb

200ml (7 fl oz) olive oil

600ml (1 pint) single cream

1 smoked pheasant

salt and freshly ground black pepper

200ml (7 fl oz) Vinaigrette Dressing (see p. 177)

mixed salad greens

120g (4½oz) cooked green beans, diced

Place the lentils and water in a large pan, bring to the boil and simmer for 5 minutes, skimming the scum which comes to the surface. Add the carrot, leek, onion, parsley and thyme and simmer for 20 minutes.

Pre-heat the oven to Gas Mark ½/120°C/250°F.

Separate the garlic cloves by putting the bulb in a pot of cold water. Bring to the boil and simmer for 5 minutes. Refresh under cold water. Peel the cloves and place in a casserole with the oil. Roast in the oven for 1 hour.

Drain the lentils. Add the cream and 3 garlic cloves.

Take the meat off the smoked pheasant carcase. Slice the breast meat thinly and dice the leg meat. Arrange the meat on a baking tray and season with salt and pepper and a little of the vinaigrette. Pop the pheasant into the pre-heated oven to warm slightly.

Toss the salad greens lightly in the remaining vinaigrette and arrange in the centre of the plate. Spoon some of the creamed lentils around the salad and sprinkle on the diced green beans and roast garlic. Take the warmed pheasant and arrange it attractively on top of the salad and serve while the lentils and pheasant are still warm.

COD FILLET WITH SMOKED GARLIC AND PARSLEY BUTTER

FLAVOURING SAUCES OR SOUPS WITH LITTLE SCRAPS OF SMOKED FISH OR MEAT ADDS
A WONDERFUL SAVOURY TANG AND DEPTH OF FLAVOUR, SO DON'T THROW OUT THOSE TRIMMINGS.
FREEZE THEM TO PERK UP YOUR NEXT DINNER PARTY DISH.

SERVES 4

4 × 200g (7oz) thick cod
fillets

salt and freshly ground white
pepper

100g (4oz) plain flour

2 tablespoons vegetable oil

FOR THE PARSLEY BUTTER

150g (5oz) unsalted butter

50g (2oz) smoked salmon
trimmings

3 garlic cloves, crushed

1 small bunch fresh parsley

3 tablespoons lemon juice

FOR THE VEGETABLES

150g (5oz) carrots, diced

150g (5oz) leeks, diced

150g (5oz) potatoes, peeled
and diced

To make the parsley butter, melt the butter in a small pan with the smoked salmon trimmings (use the lean pieces from the smoky outside trim of the salmon) and crushed garlic. Cook gently for about 10 minutes or until the butter has clarified. Allow the butter to rest off the heat for 30 minutes to let the flavours infuse.

Meanwhile, pick the parsley leaves off the stalks and blanch the leaves in boiling water for 1 minute. Refresh under very cold water, drain and roughly chop with a large knife.

Strain the clarified butter through a fine sieve, add the lemon juice and salt and pepper.

Blanch or steam the vegetables until tender then refresh them under cold water and set aside.

To cook the fillets, season them with salt and pepper then dredge them in the flour, shaking off the excess. Heat the vegetable oil in a large frying-pan until almost smoking, add a knob of fresh butter and the cod fillets. Cook over medium heat for about 4 minutes on each side. Be careful not to treat the fillets roughly or they will tend to break up.

To serve, warm the vegetables and the parsley in the parsley butter. Spoon this mixture on to warm plates and simply top with the cod.

OVERLEAF

Left: *Smoked Pheasant Salad
with Creamed Lentils and
Roast Garlic* (page 24)

Right: *Smoked Salmon and
Wheaten Bread Millefeuille
with Marinated Red Onion*
(page 30)

Smoked Haddock Tartlette with Watercress and Mustard Hollandaise

PAUL GREW UP EATING SMOKED HADDOCK AND HAS ALWAYS LOVED IT. RECENTLY, WE'VE NOTICED IT ON A FEW FANCY PARIS MENUS WHICH IS GREAT AND JUST REMINDS US NOT TO TAKE THE SIMPLE THINGS FOR GRANTED. PUFF PASTRY ALSO WORKS WELL WITH THIS RECIPE.

SERVES 4

1 quantity Savoury Shortcrust Pastry (see p. 181)

750g (1½lb) naturally smoked haddock

600ml (1 pint) milk

salt

1 bunch watercress

2 tablespoons unsalted butter

FOR THE HOLLANDAISE

3 egg yolks

1 teaspoon cold water

250g (9oz) unsalted butter, chilled and finely diced

1 teaspoon lemon juice

1 tablespoon hot Dijon mustard

salt and freshly ground white pepper

Pre-heat the oven to Gas Mark 6/200°C/400°F. Grease 4 × 10cm (4in) tartlette tins.

Roll out the pastry and use to line the prepared tartlette tins. Cover with greaseproof paper and fill with baking beans and bake in the pre-heated oven for 10–15 minutes until cooked. Remove the paper and beans.

To make the hollandaise, place the yolks and cold water in a non-reactive pan and place over a bain-marie or pan half full of simmering water. Whisk until the egg yolks are smooth and thick. Whisk in the cold, diced butter, a spoonful at a time until all the butter has been absorbed and the sauce looks thick and creamy. Season with lemon juice, mustard, salt and pepper. Leave to stand over a pan of warm water; the sauce must not be allowed to get too hot.

Trim the haddock fillets, removing all the bones care-fully. Pour the milk into a wide pan and bring to a simmer. The milk needs to be seasoned with salt but the amount really depends on how salty the smoked fillets are, as this really does vary depending on the source of the product. Place the fillets in the milk, lightly cover with greaseproof and poach for 3–4 minutes. Allow them to cool in the milk. When they are cool enough to handle, peel off the skin and break the haddock flesh into large flakes on to a microwave-safe dish (if you have a microwave) or a heatproof dish. Set aside.

Pick through the water-cress, removing the stems and any yellow leaves. Wash and then drop into boiling salted water. Strain immediately and cool quickly under cold water. Squeeze gently until the watercress is almost dry and place it on the plate with the haddock. Dot the watercress with butter and then cover with cling film (if you are using a microwave) or foil.

Re-heat the fish and watercress in the microwave for 1 minute on High or for about 5 minutes over a pan of simmering water.

Warm the tartlette bases in the oven. Spoon the watercress evenly into the tartlette bases, top with the smoked haddock, then a generous dollop of hollandaise. Serve immediately.

WARM PASTA SALAD WITH SMOKED SALMON AND FRESH HERBS

THIS IS A BEAUTIFUL LIGHT DISH FOR A SUMMER LUNCH. ONCE YOU BECOME FAMILIAR WITH IT YOU CAN BE CREATIVE, CHANGING BOTH THE PASTA TYPE AND THE GARNISHES TO SUIT YOUR MOOD.

SERVES 6

450g (1lb) dried pasta (conchiglie, penne, or fusilli)

150ml (5 fl oz) light olive oil

150ml (5 fl oz) sour cream

3 tablespoons lemon juice

salt and freshly ground white pepper

150g (5oz) Cos lettuce, washed, trimmed and shredded

250g (9oz) smoked salmon, thinly sliced and cut into 1cm ($\frac{1}{2}$ in) dice

2 tablespoons chives, finely snipped

1 tablespoon dill, roughly chopped

In a large pot, bring 5 litres (9 pints) of water to a rolling boil. Add the pasta, and cook for about 10 minutes, or until 'al dente'. Drain the pasta and place in a large serving bowl. Add the olive oil, sour cream, lemon juice, plenty of salt and pepper and toss well.

Allow to cool slightly for 5 minutes, then add the Cos lettuce, smoked salmon and the herbs. Toss gently and serve immediately.

SMOKED SALMON AND WHEATEN BREAD MILLEFEUILLE WITH MARINATED RED ONION

SMOKED SALMON AND WHEATEN BREAD ARE CONSUMED IN VAST QUANTITIES ALL OVER IRELAND. THIS IS OUR VERSION WHICH IS REALLY JUST A FANCY, DOUBLE-DECKER SANDWICH; IT'S GREAT THOUGH! A COARSE STONEGROUND WHOLEMEAL IS THE BEST BREAD TO USE.

SERVES 4

1 red onion, finely chopped

1 tablespoon rice wine vinegar

1 tablespoon Sugar Syrup (see p. 187

200g (7oz) wheaten bread

300g (11oz) smoked salmon

50g (2oz) full-fat soft cheese

2 tablespoons crème fraîche

1 small bunch fresh chives, finely snipped

3 tablespoons double cream

juice of $\frac{1}{4}$ lemon

salt

1 bunch mustard cress

$\frac{1}{2}$ cucumber, peeled, seeded and thinly sliced

4 radishes, thinly sliced

a few mixed salad leaves

$1\frac{1}{2}$ tablespoons extra virgin olive oil

Marinate the finely chopped onion in the rice wine vinegar and sugar syrup for 5–10 minutes.

Slice the wheaten bread into 12 × 5mm ($\frac{1}{4}$in) squares. Slice the smoked salmon into 12 even slices.

Mix together the full-fat soft cheese and the *crème fraîche*. Spread each slice of wheaten bread with the cheese mixture. Lay the slices of smoked salmon on top of 8 slices of wheaten bread. Sprinkle the 8 slices with the marinated chopped onion.

Start to build 4 *millefeuille* by placing the bread in layers. Top each one with the remaining 4 slices of wheaten bread and finish with the finely snipped chives.

To make the dressing, mix the cream with the lemon juice and salt.

Place the *millefeuilles* on plates and arrange around them the mustard cress, thinly sliced cucumber and radishes, and salad leaves. Drizzle with the cream dressing and the olive oil.

CHAPTER

3

THE RIVER

IRELAND IS CRISS-CROSSED with a lattice of rivers. They
start up in the rugged regions of inland hills and
mountains and work their way through the countryside to the many loughs and the coastal waters.

Fed by both springs and the frequent rain, these rivers
are host to a variety of fish. The two most commonly
sought after are the salmon and the trout. As a country
relatively undisturbed by the ravages of modern industry,
Ireland offers up some of the very best salmon fishing
rivers in Europe. The most prolific of these is the Moy in
County Mayo. Others nearby are also prosperous: the
Easky and the Palmerston, the Newport and the Bal-
lisodare to mention just a few. Indeed, there are few areas
in the world today where there is such a wealth of angling
rivers so close together, offering such diversity and
promise. For trout, it is usually the Nenagh and the
Ollatrim in County Tipperary that leap to mind, or the
Nore in County Laios. There are far too many, in fact, to
try to list here, but just speak to any angling enthusiast
and without a doubt, Ireland's rivers and their bounty
will come up in conversation.

The salmon must be the most universally esteemed
and highly regarded of fish. It is truly a gourmet food,

loved for its delicate flavour yet firm flesh. It is certainly one of the most versatile fish. It can be grilled or poached, whole or in steaks or fillets. It makes wonderful mousses, lends itself to pasta, quiches, fish cakes, and salads and salmon mayonnaise must be one of the most delightful sandwich fillers. It is good hot or cold, but just remember to let its exquisite flavour speak for itself, don't over-power it with strong ingredients.

We think most would agree that trout, brown trout in particular, is at its best when it is simply cooked: a simple fry with a little butter and a squeeze of lemon. But this does not mean that it doesn't lend itself to other flavours. Baked and stuffed, cooked *en papillote*, grilled or potted, there are many classic methods for cooking this tasty fish.

So even if you yourself are not an eager angler, don't let that stop you from enjoying some of these recipes, all of which keep clean, simple flavours in mind, ones that will let these two fish really speak for themselves.

MARINATED SALMON SALAD WITH LIME AND PICKLED GINGER

AN ORIENTAL VERSION OF CEVICHE, PREPARED WITH SALMON, THIS DISH IS LIGHT
YET VERY SATISFYING AND COULD BE SERVED AS A SUMMER MAIN COURSE.

SERVES 4

450g (1lb) fresh salmon fillet

juice of 3 limes

1 teaspoon salt

2 teaspoons caster sugar

2 heads little gem lettuce, sliced

2 tablespoons chopped fresh coriander

2 tablespoons pickled ginger (preferably Japanese) finely sliced

FOR THE SESAME GINGER VINAIGRETTE

2 tablespoons finely grated ginger root

50ml (2 fl oz) rice wine vinegar

2 tablespoons dark soy sauce

salt and freshly ground white pepper

100ml ($3\frac{1}{2}$ fl oz) sesame oil (oriental)

100ml ($3\frac{1}{2}$ fl oz) vegetable oil

TO GARNISH

pickled ginger
a few sprigs of fresh coriander

To marinate the salmon, trim the fresh salmon fillet very well, cutting away any brown parts and making sure there are no bones. Slice the fillet into about 16 thin slices and lay these into a ceramic or stainless steel dish.

Whisk the lime juice, salt and sugar together in a small bowl then pour it over the salmon pieces. Allow this to marinate for 5–10 minutes, depending on how 'cooked' you prefer your salmon. The longer it marinates, the less raw the salmon will look and it will turn lighter, a result of the marinade 'cooking' the fish.

To make the vinaigrette, combine all the ingredients except the oils together in a bowl and whisk until the salt has dissolved. Slowly whisk in the oils, a drop at a time, and taste for seasoning. This vinaigrette will not emulsify completely.

To serve, toss the lettuce slices, coriander and pickled ginger with a little of the vinaigrette. Divide between the serving plates arranging neatly by pressing the salad into 10cm (4in) cooking ring. Drain the salmon slices and place on top of the salad. Garnish with a little rosette of pickled ginger and a sprig of fresh coriander.

SALMON APPETIZERS

THIS IS REALLY THREE DISHES MASQUERADING AS ONE. EACH IS SUFFICIENTLY GOOD TO STAND UP
BY ITSELF, BUT TOGETHER, WITH A LIGHT HAND, IT BECOMES A LUXURIOUS EXTRAVAGANZA!

SERVES 6

FOR THE SALMON AND PRAWN
SAUSAGE

300g (11oz) fresh salmon
fillet

1 egg white

150ml (5 fl oz) whipping
cream

salt and freshly ground white
pepper

150g (5oz) fresh cooked
prawn meat

1 tablespoon snipped fresh
chives

1 tablespoon chopped fresh
parsley

FOR THE SMOKED SALMON

6 thin slices smoked salmon,
each about 25g (1oz)

a few mixed salad leaves

2 tablespoons Vinaigrette
Dressing (see p. 177)

FOR THE SALMON, AVOCADO
AND SUN-DRIED TOMATO
VINAIGRETTE

350g (12oz) salmon fillet

6 sun-dried tomatoes in oil

120ml (4 fl oz) Vinaigrette
Dressing (see p. 177)

1 avocado

juice of $\frac{1}{2}$ lemon

salt and freshly ground white
pepper

1 tablespoon vegetable oil

TO GARNISH

6 tablespoons Basil
Mayonnaise (see p. 53)

a few sprigs of fresh chervil
and dill

To make the salmon and prawn sausage, cut the salmon into 5mm ($\frac{1}{4}$in) dice with a sharp knife. Reserve half in a small bowl. Chill the other half and chill a bowl or food processor bowl. Put the chilled salmon in the chilled bowl with the egg white. If the ingredients are not cold the mousse will separate when the cream is added. Blend the ingredients together or pulse in the food processor until very smooth. Add the cream, salt and pepper and blend again until the cream is incorporated. Tip the mousse mixture into a bowl and stir in the reserved diced salmon. Add the prawns, chives and parsley and salt and pepper to taste. Mix together well.

To form the sausages, place a piece of cling film 30 × 46cm (12 × 18in) on a work surface. Spoon half the filling on to one end of the cling film and form into a large sausage shape. Pull the film over the sausage and twist both ends to seal and tighten the sausage. Repeat with the other half of the mixture.

To cook the sausages, place them in a steamer basket over boiling water for 8 minutes (or poach them in salted water for 10 minutes). Allow them to cool then unwrap and cut into 1cm ($\frac{1}{2}$in) slices at 45° angle. Set aside.

To prepare the smoked salmon, cut out any brown parts from the salmon. Shape the slices into neat rosette-type shapes. Break the salad leaves into small pieces and toss in the vinaigrette. Set both the rosettes and the salad aside.

To prepare the salmon with avocado and sun-dried tomato vinaigrette, cut the salmon into 6 pieces. Chop the sun-dried tomatoes then purée them in a blender with the vinaigrette. Peel the avocado, slice into 12 pieces and toss with the lemon juice.

Season the salmon with salt and pepper then heat the oil and fry it gently over quite high heat for just 3 minutes on each side. Remove from the heat.

To assemble the dish, put a little of the tossed salad in the middle of each of the 6 plates and set a rosette of smoked salmon at the top of each plate at 12 o'clock (beside the salad, not on top of it). Spoon some sun-dried tomato vinaigrette on to each plate at 4 o'clock and arrange a piece of sautéed salmon on top of this. Set 2 slices of avocado in between the smoked salmon and the sautéed salmon. Fan 3 pieces of sausage at 8 o'clock and finally, on each plate between the smoked salmon and the sausage, spoon a neat dollop of basil mayonnaise. Garnish with fresh herbs and serve.

PERFECT SALMON WITH A SIMPLE SAUCE

So many people ask us for a recipe for a tasty sauce to go with fish. Well, this is it. It's a base sauce which can be jazzed up with any amount of interesting herbs or flavourings.

SERVES 6

1 side of fresh salmon, about
1.5kg (3lb), skinned and
boned

2 tablespoons vegetable oil

salt and freshly ground white
pepper

FOR THE SAUCE

200g (7oz) unsalted butter,
chilled and diced

2 shallots, finely chopped

250ml (8 fl oz) dry white wine

100ml (4 fl oz) whipping
cream

salt and freshly ground white
pepper

To make the sauce, melt a little of the butter and fry the shallots gently for about 2 minutes over medium heat until they are soft and transparent. Add the wine, bring to the boil and boil until it has reduced to about 4 tablespoons of liquid. Pour in the cream and boil again for 1 minute. Lower the heat to low and start to whisk in the butter, a tablespoon at a time. Continue to whisk until all the butter has been incorporated.

If the sauce seems too thick, add a little water and if it seems too thin, boil it carefully to reduce slightly (you must be careful if you do this, because of the high butter content). Season with salt and freshly ground white pepper and set aside just near the stove top, in a warm but not at all hot place.

Ask your fishmonger for a skinless, boneless side of fresh salmon. You should probably order this at least 4 hours before you plan to pick it up. Check to see if he has also removed the small pin bones in the middle of the fish, above the belly. If not, remove them yourself with a small pair of pliers. Paul usually trims the meat off the belly and the tail of the salmon (freeze it for a quiche or something), just using the thickest sections. This ensures even cooking. Portion it by cutting the side into 6 even slices.

Heat a heavy frying-pan with the vegetable oil. Season the salmon fillets with salt and pepper and place carefully in the pan. If it is not hot enough, the salmon slices will stick. Cook over medium heat for 4 minutes without moving the slices then turn them over and cook for another 3 minutes. They should be ready; you can take a peek inside by opening the flesh with a spatula or your fingers. If it is still a little pink, cook for another minute.

Serve on heated plates with just about any vegetable accompaniment you like and a good ladle of the sauce.

TROUT FILLETS WITH TOMATO COMPOTE, CHERVIL AND OLIVE OIL

MAKE THIS DISH IN LATE SUMMER WHEN WILD TROUT IS IN SEASON, TOMATOES ARE AT THEIR BEST AND THE CHERVIL IS YOUNG AND FRAGRANT.

SERVES 4

4 trout fillets, about 175g (6oz) each

150ml (5 fl oz) dry white wine

1 teaspoon olive oil

1 teaspoon salt

FOR THE TOMATO COMPOTE

2 shallots, finely chopped

$\frac{1}{2}$ garlic clove, finely chopped

2 tablespoons light olive oil

1 teaspoon tomato purée

6 plum tomatoes, skinned, seeded and coarsely chopped

salt and freshly ground white pepper

FOR THE CHERVIL DRESSING

1 small bunch fresh chervil

$\frac{1}{4}$ teaspoon salt

juice of 1 lemon

150ml (5 fl oz) virgin olive oil

To make the tomato compote, fry the shallots and garlic gently in oil for about 2 minutes over medium heat. Add the tomato purée, the chopped plum tomatoes and a little salt and pepper. Bring to the boil quickly and simmer for 2 minutes. Remove from the heat.

To make the chervil dressing, pick the chervil leaves off their stalks, reserve the stalks and coarsely chop the leaves. In a small bowl, mix the salt and some freshly ground white pepper with the lemon juice and then stir in the oil. Finally, stir in the chopped chervil. Set aside.

To cook the trout, carefully trim the trout fillets. Scale them with a blunt, serrated knife and try to take out any small bones with a pair of pliers. Rinse the fillets in cold water and drain in a colander.

Place the wine in a wide saucepan with the reserved chervil stalks, oil and salt and bring to the boil. Carefully put the trout fillets into the wine, cover and simmer very gently for 2 minutes. Remove from the heat and allow to stand for 1 minute before serving.

Spoon the tomato compote on to warmed plates and drizzle each plate with the chervil oil dressing. Quickly place a trout fillet on each plate and serve immediately.

OVERLEAF

Left: *Perfect Salmon with a Simple Sauce* (page 36)

Right: *Trout Fillets with Tomato Compote, Chervil and Olive Oil*

GRATIN OF TROUT WITH CUCUMBER RIBBONS AND DILL

IT'S GOOD TO LEARN THIS SIMPLE LITTLE GRATIN TECHNIQUE WHICH CAN BE APPLIED TO ANY MEAT OR FISH DISH WITH A CREAM SAUCE. IF YOU DON'T HAVE A GRILL THE DISH WILL TASTE FINE WITHOUT IT.

SERVES 4

4 trout fillets, 200g (7oz) each

salt and freshly ground white pepper

1 cucumber

2 tablespoons unsalted butter

4 tablespoons water

FOR THE SAUCE

4 shallots, thinly sliced

250ml (8 fl oz) dry Riesling

250ml (8 fl oz) double cream

1 tablespoon Dijon mustard

1 small bunch fresh dill, picked and chopped

100ml (4 fl oz) whipping cream, whipped to soft peaks

Pre-heat the grill to 200°C/400°F.

To make the sauce, combine the shallots and wine in a small pan and boil over moderately high heat until reduced to about 6 tablespoons of liquid. Add the double cream and boil gently until it thickens to sauce consistency. Strain through a fine mesh sieve into a clean pan and reserve in a warm place while you prepare the trout.

To prepare the trout, trim and scale the trout fillets. Check that all the bones have been removed and cut each fillet into 6 diamond-shaped pieces. (Simply cut the fillet across following the angle at the top of the fillet.) Season with salt and pepper and arrange in a steaming basket. Steam for 2 minutes.

While the fish is steaming, prepare the cucumber ribbons. Peel the cucumber and discard the skin. Now, using the peeler, take long ribbon-like strips of the cucumber until you reach the seeds. Continue doing this until you have made ribbons with the whole cucumber.

Melt the butter in a pan with the water. Add the cucumber ribbons, some salt and pepper and cook over high heat, for about 2 minutes or until the ribbons are tender but still slightly crunchy.

To complete the dish, bring the sauce back to the boil then remove it from the heat. Whisk in the mustard and the chopped dill.

Divide the cucumber ribbons between warmed plates and spread them out to form a bed for the trout. Arrange the trout pieces on top of the cucumber, alternating each piece skin side up, skin side down, to form a mosaic-like pattern.

Fold the whipped cream into the sauce and spoon a generous amount over the trout. Place each plate under the grill for about 1 minute until it browns beautifully. Serve at once.

SUMMER SALAD ROSCOFF

This salad is inspired by the famous Salad Niçoise. I am sure that if the people of Provence were to spend time in Ireland, they would wholeheartedly approve of our substituting salmon for tuna.

SERVES 4

200ml (7 fl oz) white wine

200ml (7 fl oz) water

2 tablespoons white wine vinegar

1 bouquet garni

1 teaspoon salt

450g (1lb) boneless salmon fillet

FOR THE SALAD GARNISHES

120g (4½oz) green beans, cut into 2cm (¾in) lengthwise

4 tablespoons Mayonnaise (see page 177)

1 tablespoon fresh basil, chopped

2 anchovy fillets, finely minced

2 tablespoons poaching liquid

salt and freshly ground black pepper

120g (4½oz) mixed salad greens

4 tablespoons Vinaigrette Dressing (see page 177)

½ cucumber, peeled, quartered lengthwise and chopped

250g (9oz) tasty salad tomatoes

4 hard-boiled eggs (cooked for 9 minutes), peeled and quartered

120g (4½oz) black olives, stones removed

To cook the salmon, pour the wine, water and wine vinegar into a wide pan. Add the bouquet garni and salt and bring to the boil. Immerse the salmon fillet in the liquid, and simmer very gently for 2 minutes. Remove from the heat, cover, and allow to cool.

To prepare the salad, cook the green beans in salted boiling water for 6 minutes, and then drain. Refresh in cold water, and drain again.

To make the dressing, whisk the mayonnaise, chopped basil, and minced anchovies together in a small bowl. Thin with the poaching liquid, whisking continually. Taste for seasoning, and add salt and pepper as needed.

To serve, toss the salad leaves with the vinaigrette, and arrange attractively in the centre of each plate. Arrange the salad garnishes around. Remove the salmon from the poaching liquid, and flake carefully onto each plate. Drizzle with some of the anchovy and basil dressing.

CHAPTER

4

THE LOUGH

IRELAND HAS SOME of the largest inland lakes in the
whole of Europe. Because the country is relatively
underdeveloped and has little heavy industry, these
lakes are just teeming with fish. They attract anglers from
all over the world. Trout, pike and eel, so highly esteemed
on the Continent for centuries, are in plentiful supply.
One gilly told us the true story of how some Europeans
used to come over on fishing holidays and catch so many
pike that upon their return home they could sell their
catch (at highly inflated prices, nonetheless) and pay for
their whole holiday! Thankfully, stricter measures are
now in effect to prevent this from happening and ensure
that the lakes are not overfished.

All the fish out of Irish loughs are wonderful for eating,
even if the general population haven't yet realized this.
The main reason is because the cold waters are so free
from pollution, the fish have pure and healthy diets and
consequently bear tasty flesh in prime condition. The
people who inhabit the lakeshores know this, but still
most of the catch is air-freighted abroad to more appreci-
ative markets.

Perch has a firm white flesh with a delicate flavour.
Pike is bonier than other fish but this certainly doesn't

detract from the quality or taste. In King Henry VIII's time, pike would fetch more at the market than a lamb or chicken. The culinary reputation of eels is evident everywhere else; the Dutch, Germans and Japanese all go mad over it, whether it is smoked or fresh.

It is certainly high time that people in Britain and Ireland were encouraged to be more daring in their tastes. Perhaps it is the fault of the shops and fishmongers. If they assume there is no market because of past history and therefore do not stock it, how are people to give it a chance? We must request the delightful fish, for if there is no demand, there will be no supply.

DEEP-FRIED PERCH WITH LIGHT TARTARE SAUCE

TONS OF PERCH ARE FLOWN FROM IRELAND TO THE CONTINENT EVERY YEAR WHERE IT IS CONSUMED IN VAST QUANTITIES. THIS IS A FAVOURITE COOKING TECHNIQUE FOR THE SMALL FILLETS WHICH BOTH PROTECTS THE FISH AND BULKS IT OUT.

SERVES 4

450g (1lb) perch fillets

oil for deep-frying

salt

4 tablespoons plain flour

FOR THE BATTER

120g (4½oz) plain flour

1 tablespoon oil

200ml (7 fl oz) beer or water

salt and freshly ground white pepper

2 egg whites

FOR THE TARTARE SAUCE

250ml (8 fl oz) Mayonnaise (see page 177)

1 tablespoon finely chopped gherkins

1 tablespoon finely chopped fine capers

1 tablespoon finely chopped fresh parsley

4–6 tablespoons water (optional)

TO GARNISH

1 lemon, cut into wedges

To make the batter, sift the flour into a large bowl. Add the oil and beer or water and season with salt and pepper. Whisk the ingredients together until they are just incorporated. Leave the batter to rest for about 1 hour otherwise it will shrink when cooked. After 1 hour, beat the egg whites to a light froth and carefully fold into the batter.

To make the tartare sauce, simply combine the mayonnaise with the gherkins, capers and parsley. Dilute with the water if you desire a lighter sauce which will spread on the plate.

To cook the perch fillets, pre-heat the oil in a deep pan or deep-fat fryer to about 180°C/350°F when a cube of bread will turn golden in 1 minute. Season the perch fillets with salt and coat lightly with the flour, shaking off any excess.

Dip the fillets into the batter then cook in the hot oil for about 3 minutes or until golden brown. Remove from the pan and transfer to kitchen paper to drain off excess fat.

To serve, spread a little of the tartare sauce over each plate and divide the perch fillets evenly between them. Serve at once with a wedge of lemon and some chips or salad on the side.

Japanese-Style Barbecued Eel with Stir-fried Vegetables

This technique is called *kabayaki* and it is very popular in Japan.
Eel lends itself well to *teriyaki* style of flavours, as do many other foods, so try
this recipe with chicken or pork, too.

SERVES 4

5 tablespoons dark soy sauce

120ml (4 fl oz) mirin (cooking saké) or sherry

2 eels, skinned, cleaned and cut into 7.5cm (3in) slices

2 tablespoons vegetable oil

FOR THE STIR-FRIED VEGETABLES

2 sticks celery, peeled and diagonally sliced

120g (4½oz) shiitake mushrooms

1 red pepper, cut into strips

120g (4½oz) mangetouts

1 head bok choy, cut into 4cm (1½in) pieces

1 tablespoon vegetable oil

1 teaspoon chopped garlic

1 teaspoon chopped fresh ginger root

salt and freshly ground black pepper

1 teaspoon dark sesame oil

1 small bunch fresh coriander

2 tablespoons sesame seeds, toasted

To cook the eels, boil the soy sauce and *mirin* together in a small pan until it has reduced to about 6 tablespoons.

Heat the barbecue or grill. When it is nice and hot, place the eel fillets on a grilling rack, oil them lightly and place the rack on the barbecue. Grill them for about 5 minutes each side. Then start to baste them with the reduction of *mirin* and soy sauce. Continue to grill them for another 10 minutes, basting frequently.

To stir-fry the vegetables, blanch each of the vegetables in a pan of boiling, salted water for about 30 seconds or until they have just about lost that raw crunch. Allow them to drain.

Heat the vegetable oil in a large wok or frying-pan until almost smoking. Add the garlic and ginger, stir briefly and then stir in the vegetables. Cook for about 45 seconds then season with salt and pepper and the sesame oil.

To serve, arrange the stir-fried vegetables in the centre of warmed plates. Place 3 pieces of eel attractively on top of the vegetables. Sprinkle with fresh coriander and sesame seeds.

SAUTÉED PIKE WITH CRAYFISH AND GARLIC VINAIGRETTE

A PIKE FROM A CLEAN, PURE LOUGH IS A GREAT FISH TO EAT. IT WILL NOT HAVE THE COARSE TASTE THAT YOU MAY ASSOCIATE WITH RIVER PIKE. IT'S GREAT FOR THIS RECIPE BECAUSE IT HAS ENOUGH FLAVOUR TO STAND UP TO THE GARLIC IN THE VINAIGRETTE. YOU CAN USE ROACH OR OTHER WHITE FISH AS AN ALTERNATIVE.

SERVES 6

1.5kg (3lb) live freshwater crayfish

6 pike fillets, each 175g (6oz)

salt and freshly ground white pepper

2 tablespoons oil

2 tablespoons unsalted butter

FOR THE SAUCE

3 tablespoons oil

2 tablespoons chopped carrot

2 tablespoons chopped onion

2 garlic cloves

1 tablespoon tomato purée

2 tablespoons brandy

100ml (4 fl oz) dry white wine

1 litre (1¾ pints) water

300ml (10 fl oz) double cream

FOR THE VINAIGRETTE

2 plum tomatoes

200ml (7 fl oz) Vinaigrette Dressing (see p. 177)

1 teaspoon crushed garlic

1 teaspoon chopped fresh tarragon

1 teaspoon chopped fresh parsley

TO GARNISH

a few sprigs fresh tarragon and chervil

To cook the crayfish, bring 5 litres (9 pints) of salted water to the boil. Wash the crayfish under running water then plunge them into the boiling water. Let the water return to the boil and then simmer for just 30 seconds. Switch off the heat and let the pan stand for 4 minutes. Drain and refresh the crayfish in cold water. Separate the heads from the tails, reserving the heads for the sauce, and peel the tails. Set aside.

To make the sauce, crush the crayfish heads in a large bowl with a wooden spoon.

Heat the oil until smoking in a very large pan, toss in the crushed crayfish and fry over high heat for 3 minutes, stirring. Add the chopped vegetables and garlic and cook for another 2 minutes. Add the tomato purée, brandy and wine and boil until the wine has reduced by half. Add the water, reduce the heat and simmer for 20 minutes.

Strain the sauce through a

fine sieve into a clean pan, and discard the heads. Boil to reduce the sauce until you have about 250ml (8 fl oz) of concentrated juices left. Add the cream and boil until it is thick and creamy.

To make the garlic vinaigrette, blanch the tomatoes in a pan of boiling water for 10 seconds. Transfer them immediately into cold water. Peel off the skin, cut them in half and squeeze out the seeds. Carefully cut the remaining flesh into neat 1cm ($\frac{1}{2}$in) dice.

In a bowl, whisk together the vinaigrette, garlic and herbs. Finally, stir in the tomato dice.

To cook the pike, remove any bones with a sharp knife and give the fillets a nice shape. Skin the fillets if this has not already been done. Season with salt and pepper.

Heat the oil in a large, heavy-based frying-pan until it is almost smoking. Add the butter and as it begins to foam, add the fillets. Fry for about 3 minutes on each side. Press the fillets gently; if they want to flake apart, they are cooked and ready.

To serve, warm the crayfish tails in the vinaigrette in a small pan. Spoon equal quantities of the vinaigrette, crayfish tails and then the cream sauce on to warmed plates. Carefully place a fillet in the centre of each, garnish with sprigs of tarragon and chervil.

FRESHWATER FISH CAKES
WITH SPRING ONIONS

THIS IS A SUPER RECIPE FOR USING UP BITS AND PIECES OF FISH OR SHELLFISH.
MADE WITH FRESHWATER FISH, WELL YOU CAN HARDLY TASTE THE DIFFERENCE.

SERVES 4

500g (1lb 2oz) fresh boneless
fillets of pike, roach or perch

100g (4oz) spring onions,
finely chopped

100ml (3½fl oz) Mayonnaise
(see p. 177)

100g (4oz) fresh
breadcrumbs, soaked in milk
and squeezed

1 egg

1 tablespoon chopped fresh
parsley

1 tablespoon chopped fresh
thyme

salt and cayenne pepper

50g (2oz) fresh breadcrumbs

50g (2oz) ground almonds

3 tablespoons oil

3 tablespoons unsalted butter

1 quantity Mustard Sauce (see
p. 64)

To prepare the fish, firstly, make sure there are no bones. If you have to, cut away the bones and discard these and any imperfect pieces of fish. Cut the fillets into thin strips and then into 5mm (¼in) dice and place in a bowl. Mix the fish with the spring onions, mayonnaise, breadcrumbs, egg, herbs and season with salt and cayenne pepper.

Divide the mixture into 12 portions and form each into a neat patty, about 9cm (3½in) in diameter. Mix together the breadcrumbs and ground almonds and dredge each fish cake in the mixture, patting to coat evenly with the crumbs.

Heat a little oil in a heavy frying-pan and add the butter. When it foams, add 6 of the fish cakes. Cover and cook over medium high heat for about 3 minutes on each side. Transfer the cakes on to kitchen paper while you cook the other 6 cakes.

Serve with a small salad and the mustard sauce.

SALAD OF SMOKED EEL WITH BEETROOT AND CHIVES

GOOD SMOKED EEL IS A REALLY GREAT FOOD PRODUCT WELL WORTH TRYING.
BUY IT WHOLE WITH THE SKIN ON TO ENSURE FRESHNESS.

SERVES 4

2 medium-sized beetroot, washed and trimmed

1 smoked eel, whole with skin on

1 tablespoon Dijon mustard

150ml (5 fl oz) Vinaigrette Dressing (see p. 177)

salt and freshly ground white pepper

4 tablespoons double cream

1 tablespoon lemon juice

1 small bunch fresh chives, snipped

a few mixed salad leaves

If you have a microwave, wrap the beetroot in cling film and cook in a microwave at full power for about 12 minutes. Allow to rest for about 5 minutes. Unwrap the beetroot and with kitchen paper, simply push the skins off. Otherwise you can boil the beetroot in water for 30–60 minutes until tender, depending on size. Push off the skins. Cut the beetroot into neat 5mm ($\frac{1}{4}$in) slices.

Whisk the mustard into the vinaigrette and marinate the beetroot slices with a little salt and pepper in half the vinaigrette mixture for at least 30 minutes.

To prepare the eel, pull the head back, breaking the backbone off the neck. Pull the head towards the tail to free the skin and pull it off. Now run a small knife down both sides of the backbone. Pry the flesh away from the bone with your fingers, releasing any tricky bits again with your knife. Cut the fillets into 6cm ($2\frac{1}{2}$in) pieces and set aside.

Mix the cream, lemon juice, chives and a little salt and pepper.

To serve, toss the salad leaves with some of the remaining vinaigrette and arrange them in the centre of each plate. Arrange the beetroot in 3 piles around the salad and place pieces of smoked eel in between these piles. Drizzle each plate generously with the chive cream.

CHAPTER

5

THE SHORELINE

THE WESTERN SEABOARD of Ireland must be one of the world's most unpolluted stretches of coastline. All around her coast is truly a region of plenty. Cockles and mussels, oysters, scallops, prawns and lobsters; it is a pure and plentiful harvest awaiting anyone that goes in search.

Although Molly Malone has preached about the wonderful cockles and mussels here for years, they are still vastly under-rated and under-used locally. Lorries arrive from the Continent on a daily basis to take them back to Spain and France by the ton. Obviously, the people there have a developed taste for these molluscs and perhaps, as more locals visit these countries, they too will develop an appreciation for them. They definitely deserve it.

Thankfully, there is more local interest in some of the other shellfish. Oysters have always enjoyed a great following here. Indeed, there are several festivals throughout Ireland paying homage to these delicacies. The Galway Festival is perhaps the best known. Every September the town is absolutely engulfed by people, there to consume in great quantity the famous local oysters along with plenty of brown bread and Guinness. What could be better?

All around the coast, restaurants have, especially in recent years, taken to serving more crabs, Dublin Bay prawns and of course, the lobster. Needless to say, simple treatment is all that is necessary if these products are fresh and in season. Boiling Dublin Bay prawns or lobster and serving them with fresh butter can be one of the most satisfying and memorable meals possible. Indeed, simple preparation actually suits most shellfish best. It

lets their wonderful flavour speak for itself. However, they all lend themselves to soups and chowders, pastas, rice dishes, risotto, puff pastry, pies, salads and just about anything else one could dream up. Just be sure to start with a fresh product, don't make the usual mistake of overcooking, and you will undoubtedly come up with a winner of a dish.

CLAM CHOWDER WITH POTATOES AND DULSE

CHOWDER IS A WONDERFUL HEARTY SOUP AVAILABLE IN ALMOST EVERY SEASIDE TOWN IN THE UNITED STATES. WE LOVE IT, AND IN IRELAND WE HAVE ALL THE KEY INGREDIENTS, SO DON'T HESITATE TO GIVE IT A GO. DULSE IS DRIED SEAWEED AND IS AVAILABLE IN DELICATESSENS.

SERVES 4–6

1kg (2lb 4oz) fresh live clams

25g (1oz) dried dulse

2 tablespoons chopped onion

2 tablespoons chopped leek

2 tablespoons chopped carrot

1 sprig of fresh parsley

1 sprig of fresh thyme

400ml (14 fl oz) water

175ml (6 fl oz) dry white wine

1 medium onion, finely chopped

200g (7oz) streaky bacon, rinded and chopped

2 tablespoons unsalted butter

250ml (8 fl oz) fish stock, light chicken stock or water

2 large potatoes, roughly diced

200ml (7 fl oz) double cream

1 tablespoon chopped fresh parsley

To prepare and cook the clams, wash them under cold running water. Finely slice or chop the dulse with a sharp knife and put it into a large pan with the other aromatics: the chopped onion, leek, carrot, parsley and thyme. Add the water, bring to the boil and simmer for 10 minutes to infuse the flavours. Add the wine and return to the boil.

Add the clams, cover and boil vigorously for 1–2 minutes until the clams open. Drain them into a colander, being sure to catch the cooking liquid in a bowl underneath. This will be used in the chowder. Set aside while you pull the clams from their shells. Discard the shells and the sprigs of parsley and thyme. Keep the clams and the aromatics and place them in the reserved broth.

To make the chowder, fry the onion and bacon in the 2 tablespoons of butter over a medium heat in a large pan until it is soft and transparent.

Add the stock or water and bring to a simmer. Add the potatoes to the pan and simmer gently until they are cooked.

Remove half the potato mixture and blend in a blender or food processor or mash. This will give you a thick, creamy soup which will thicken the whole chowder.

Combine the 2 potato mixtures, the clams in their juices and cooking broth and the cream and bring to a simmer. Taste for seasoning, garnish with the chopped parsley and, if desired, a dollop of whipped cream, and serve at once.

LOBSTER SALAD WITH BASIL MAYONNAISE

If you want a gourmet dish that's easy and quick to make, go no further.
It's simplicity itself and it looks and tastes stunning.

SERVES 4

1 live lobster about 750g
(1½lb)

mixed salad leaves

2 tablespoons Vinaigrette
Dressing (see p. 177)

6 red cherry tomatoes, halved

6 yellow cherry tomatoes,
halved

1 avocado, peeled and sliced

FOR THE BASIL MAYONNAISE

1 tablespoon Dijon mustard

salt and freshly ground white
pepper

1 tablespoon white wine
vinegar

3 egg yolks

500ml (17 fl oz) vegetable oil
or light olive oil

½ cup chopped fresh basil

To make the mayonnaise, whisk the mustard, salt, pepper and wine vinegar in a bowl until the salt has dissolved. Add the egg yolks and whisk in the oil, very slowly at first, literally drop by drop. As the mayonnaise starts to build up, you can add the oil slightly faster but always be sure to incorporate each addition fully before adding more. Add the chopped basil and taste for seasoning. Do not add the basil until the last moment or so before serving because the basil will lose its colour if it is done too far in advance.

To kill the lobster, place it on a board and cover the foil with a cloth. Hold firmly with one hand and with the point of a large knife pierce down to the board through the cross marked on the centre of the head.

To cook the lobster heat a large pan of water to a vigorous boil. Put the lobster in and let it cook for about 14 minutes. Stop the cooking process by plunging the lobster into a pot of ice cold water.

Insert a knife into the lobster at the point where the tail and body are joined and cut towards the tail. The tail meat will now easily pull away from the shell. Break off the claws and crack the shells with a heavy knife. Remove the meat from the claws, being careful to discard any pieces of shell. Slice up the meat neatly.

To serve, toss the mixed salad in the vinaigrette and pile in the centre of each plate. Surround in an attractive manner with the cherry tomatoes, the avocado slices and finally the lobster meat. Spoon the basil mayonnaise on to the plate, either in one generous dollop or, if you prefer, drizzle over the lobster and salad. Serve immediately.

OVERLEAF

Left: *Lobster Salad with Basil*
Mayonnaise

Right: *Steamed Symphony of*
Seafood with Saffron Butter
Vinaigrette (page 69)

CRISPY PRAWN SPRING ROLLS WITH A SPICED CORIANDER SALSA

WE JUST LOVE CHINESE FOOD AND RESPECT THEIR OBSESSION WITH FRESHNESS. FOR THIS RECIPE WE USE LOCAL LIVE PRAWNS, ORGANIC CABBAGE AND FRESH CORIANDER. RAW PRAWNS WILL GIVE YOU BY FAR THE BEST FLAVOUR – AND LIVE ONES ARE EVEN BETTER – BUT IF YOU HAVE TO USE COOKED PRAWNS, CHOOSE THE BEST QUALITY AND OMIT THE COOKING STAGE.

SERVES 4

16 large fresh raw prawns

2 tablespoons vegetable oil

$\frac{1}{4}$ head Savoy cabbage, thinly sliced

100g (4oz) shiitake mushrooms, thinly sliced

1 teaspoon chopped fresh ginger root

1 garlic clove

1 teaspoon sesame oil

salt and freshly ground white pepper

4 large spring roll wrappers, cut in 4 squares to give 16 pieces

2 egg yolks for sealing

1 litre ($1\frac{3}{4}$ pints) vegetable oil for deep-frying

FOR THE SALSA

1 yellow pepper, peeled, seeded and diced

1 red pepper, peeled, seeded and diced

1 tablespoon vegetable oil

2 plum tomatoes, skinned, seeded and diced

2 tablespoons rice wine vinegar

1 tablespoon sugar

1 tablespoon tomato ketchup

1 tablespoon snipped fresh chives

2 tablespoons chopped fresh coriander

Cook the prawns in a large pan of boiling, salted water for 3 minutes. Refresh them in cold water and peel them so that you have only the fleshy tail meat. Chop this into 1cm ($\frac{1}{2}$in) dice. Set aside.

Heat the vegetable oil in a large frying-pan until it is smoking. Add the cabbage, mushrooms, ginger and the garlic. Stir-fry for exactly 1 minute and then tip into a large bowl. Allow to cool and then add the prawns and sesame oil and season with salt and pepper. Mix well.

Lay the spring roll wrappers out in a diamond shape. Arrange the mixture on the wrappers in a cylinder shape. Fold up the bottom corner over the mixture then pull in the two side corners. Roll up over the top corner and brush very lightly with the egg yolk to seal it closed. Note that it is important not to let the wrappers dry out before they are filled. Also, do not overfill them.

To make the salsa, fry the peppers in the oil over a gentle heat for 2 minutes. Add the plum tomatoes and fry gently for a further 1 minute. Add the wine vinegar, sugar, ketchup and taste for seasoning. Season with salt and pepper if necessary. Do not add the chopped chives and coriander until just before serving.

To serve, heat the oil in a large pan to approximately 180°C/350°F when a cube of bread will brown in 1 minute. Fry the spring rolls in small batches for about 5 minutes until golden brown. Drain on kitchen paper. Serve immediately with plenty of the fresh salsa on the side.

MUSSELS IN A PESTO·BROTH

THESE MUSSELS ARE DELICIOUS SERVED WITH PASTA, OR ADD A SPLASH OF
DOUBLE CREAM FOR AN ELEGANT SOUP.

SERVES 4

250ml (8 fl oz) dry white wine

100ml (3½ fl oz) water

3 tablespoons onions, finely chopped

3kg (7lb) live mussels

2 ripe tomatoes, peeled, seeded and roughly chopped

1 teaspoon cracked black pepper

3–4 tablespoons fresh Basil Pesto (see pages 116–17)

Simmer the wine, water and onion in a large pot. Meanwhile, clean the mussels by rinsing them in cold water, and pull away the hairy beard. Add the mussels to the pot, cover and boil vigorously for 1 minute. Add the tomatoes and black pepper, and boil for one more minute, or until all the mussels have opened. Discard any that remain closed.

Drain the mussels into a colander with a bowl underneath to catch the tasty broth. Reserve this. As soon as they are cool enough to handle, shell them.

Add the mussels back to the broth, and heat gently. Do not boil or the mussels will toughen. Stir in the pesto, and serve in a bowl with pasta, or just some nice crusty bread.

GRATIN OF OYSTERS WITH LEEKS AND CHARDONNAY

WE PREFER RAW OYSTERS TO COOKED. IT'S HARD TO BEAT PLAIN BUTTERED WHEATEN BREAD AND A GLASS OF GUINNESS TO GO WITH THESE BRINY CREATURES. HOWEVER, IF YOU ARE GOING TO COOK THEM, KEEP IT SIMPLE SUCH AS THIS DISH AND DON'T OVERCOOK THEM.

SERVES 4

10 oysters, removed from their shells and stored in their juices

2 small leeks

1 tablespoon unsalted butter

salt and cayenne pepper

350ml (12 fl oz) Chardonnay

350ml (12 fl oz) whipping cream

squeeze of lemon juice

TO GARNISH

snipped fresh chives

puff pastry crescent (optional)

Pre-heat the grill to hot.

Slice the leeks finely and wash if necessary. Heat the butter in a small pan with the salt and cayenne pepper and sweat the leeks over gentle heat for about 4 minutes or until tender. Tip the leeks into serving dishes to form a neat bed. Set aside.

To make the sauce, pour half the Chardonnay into a small pan. Add the juices of the oysters and boil to reduce this by two-thirds. Add half the cream and boil again until it has achieved a rich sauce consistency. Check the seasoning, add a squeeze of lemon juice, and then set aside, keeping warm.

Whip the remaining cream until it is stiff and place in the fridge for the moment.

To heat the oysters, place the remaining Chardonnay in a small pan with a little salt and bring to the boil. Immediately tip in the oysters, count to 10 and then remove from the heat. Let them continue to poach off the heat for another 30 seconds. Remove the oysters from the liquid and drain in a sieve or on paper towels. Quickly arrange the oysters on top of the leek beds and keep warm just beside the grill. Don't let the oysters get too hot or they will be rubbery.

To serve, bring the cream sauce back to the boil then add the snipped chives. Fold in the whipped cream very roughly with a spoon and then spoon this sauce over the oysters. Place the plates under a hot grill and watch carefully. After about 1–2 minutes, the cream will have browned beautifully. Top with a puff pastry crescent, if using, and serve immediately.

CHARGRILLED SCALLOPS WITH A SPAGHETTI NERI AND SAFFRON CREAM SAUCE

SCALLOPS REALLY SUIT THE CHARGRILL; IT SEEMS TO BRING OUT THEIR NATURAL SWEETNESS.
QUALITY AND FRESHNESS ARE OF THE UTMOST IMPORTANCE SO DON'T ACCEPT ONES WHICH
HAVE BEEN SOAKED IN WATER TO INCREASE THEIR SIZE.

SERVES 4

*750g (1lb 10oz) fresh
scallops, unsoaked*

2 tablespoons light olive oil

*salt and freshly ground white
pepper*

FOR THE SAFFRON SAUCE

2 shallots, finely chopped

1 garlic clove

*the trim from the scallops, or
50g (2oz) whiting, etc*

1 tablespoon unsalted butter

*200ml (7 fl oz) medium dry
white wine*

a pinch of saffron threads

250ml (8 fl oz) double cream

*salt and freshly ground black
pepper*

*250g (9oz) fresh pasta,
preferably Pasta Nera (see
p. 181)*

2 tablespoons unsalted butter

Trim the scallops, carefully removing any sand, membrane and tough muscle and any ragged edges. This trim is used in the sauce so don't throw it out. Dry the scallops on kitchen paper.

To make the sauce, fry the shallots, garlic and scallop trim in the butter over medium heat for about 4 minutes. Do not let it colour. Add the wine and the saffron and boil until the wine has reduced to about 3 tablespoons. Add the cream and simmer until the cream has reduced and thickened to sauce consistency. Season with salt and pepper and pass through a fine sieve into a clean pan. Set aside.

Cook the fresh pasta in a large pan of boiling salted water for about 1 minute until all the pasta floats to the surface. Drain the pasta and toss in the butter with a little salt and pepper. Set aside.

Toss the scallops in light olive oil with salt and pepper.

Quickly place the scallops on a very hot chargrill (alternatively, a very hot, cast-iron frying-pan). Allow them to cook and brown without touching or moving them for the first 2 minutes. Turn them over and cook them for 1 minute on the other side.

To serve arrange the pasta in the middle of warm plates. Top with the scallops and pour over and around the saffron cream sauce. Garnish with a few fresh herbs, if desired, such as chervil or flat-leaved parsley.

SPICED RAGOUT OF SHELLFISH UNDER A PUFF PASTRY LID

THE TECHNIQUE OF BAKING A SOUP UNDER A PUFF PASTRY LID HAS BEEN ABOUT FOR A WHILE.
THE WHOLE POINT IS THAT IT ADDS INTEREST AND THEN WHEN YOU BREAK THE PASTRY, YOUR
SENSES ARE OVERWHELMED BY THE WONDERFUL AROMAS.

SERVES 4

250g (9oz) Puff Pastry (see p. 182–3)

1 live lobster, about 750g (1lb 8oz)

12 large raw prawns

185g (6½oz) fresh shelled scallops

2 egg yolks to glaze

FOR SOUP BASE

25g (1oz) unsalted butter

50g (2oz) shallots, chopped

25g (1oz) fresh ginger root, chopped

120g (4½oz) celery, chopped

120g (4½oz) celeriac, chopped

450ml (15 fl oz) fish stock

120ml (4 fl oz) double cream

1 tablespoon snipped fresh chives

2 tablespoons chopped fresh coriander

1 teaspoon hot chilli powder

On a floured work surface, roll out the puff pastry to a thickness of about 3mm (⅛in). Transfer the rolled piece on to a baking sheet or tray and chill in the fridge for at least 20 minutes.

When it is again cold and firm, use your soup bowl overturned to estimate the size of the round to cut. It should be 5mm (¼in) larger in perimeter than the bowl to ensure that you will be able to seal the puff securely around the bowl. Again, place in the fridge to chill for 20 minutes.

To make the soup base, melt the butter and fry the shallots, ginger and celery in a large pan. When they are all soft, add the celeriac and the fish stock. Cook over medium heat for about 10 minutes. Add the cream and bring to the boil. Remove from the heat and purée in a blender and pass through a fine mesh sieve. Allow to cool.

To prepare the seafood, put a large pan of salted water on to boil. First blanch the lobster for about 15 minutes and remove it from the pan. Then blanch the large prawns for about 2 minutes. Refresh them in cold water and when cool enough to handle, peel off the shells, reserving them for use another time (these shells can be frozen until needed). Cut the lobster and prawns into 1cm (½in) pieces. Dice the fresh scallop meat into pieces approximately the same size.

Pre-heat the oven to Gas Mark 6/200°C/400°F.

Add the seafood to the soup along with the herbs and chilli powder. Ladle into the soup bowls. Brush the perimeter of the bowls carefully with a little of the egg yolk glaze, then top with the puff rounds and seal the edges.

Decorate the top of the puff by brushing with the glaze and then scoring very gently a pattern on the glaze.

Place the bowls on a sturdy baking sheet and cook in the pre-heated oven for about 8 minutes. Remember that the bowls will be very hot on removal from the oven and should be lifted with an oven glove on to the underplates.

GRILLED DUBLIN BAY PRAWNS WITH GARLIC BUTTER

WE ARE BLESSED IN IRELAND WITH PLENTY OF FRESH LIVE PRAWNS. BUY YOUR PRAWNS (AND LOBSTERS) ONLY FROM A RELIABLE SOURCE AS FRESHNESS IS A MOST IMPORTANT FACTOR.

SERVES 4 (AS A STARTER)

200ml (7 fl oz) dry white wine

2 shallots, finely chopped

120g (4½oz) soft unsalted butter

½-1 tablespoon garlic, minced

2 tablespoons fresh parsley, chopped

1 tablespoon fresh tarragon, chopped

2 tablespoons Pernod (optional)

salt and freshly ground white pepper

squeeze of lemon juice

12 large, very fresh whole raw prawns, preferably head on

To make the butter, boil the white wine with the shallots in a small saucepan, until reduced by half. Now blend the butter, garlic, herbs and Pernod with the white wine and shallot reduction, in a food processor until well mixed. Taste the butter carefully for salt and pepper, and add some lemon juice if you feel it needs it.

Pre-heat the grill to high.

Working on a large cutting board with a large chef's knife, split the prawns lengthwise from head to tail. Crack each claw by tapping it with the back of a knife. Arrange the prawns closely on the grill tray, open side facing upwards. Season the prawns lightly with salt and pepper, and spread the garlic butter very generously over the prawns. Cook for 5 minutes on the lowest rack of the grill. Shake the pan occasionally to prevent the butter from burning, and to mix in those wonderful juices.

Serve immediately with lots of bread for sopping up the tasty garlic butter. Paul finds the best part of this dish is sucking the shells and claws to savour every last drop of flavour.

CHAPTER

6

THE OCEAN

O NE HAS ONLY to look at Ireland's geographical
location to appreciate what a huge diversity of
seafood there is available to her fishing fleets.
The pure cold waters of the Atlantic ocean on her north
and west; the Celtic Sea to her south and the Irish Sea to
the east, all rich in fish – and some of the very best in
the world at that.

Paul truly believes that he's never seen such quality –
so fresh and so continually consistent – anywhere in the
world (at such good market prices as well). It's quite
strange then that Ireland is not really a fish-eating nation.
Perhaps with such an abundance of grass-fed animals,
domestic and wild, it didn't seem necessary to go to
sea for food. There are some traditional old-fashioned
favourites: herring, mackerel and kipper would be the
best known. Ling used to be salted and dried and sold
inland for winter use. Whiting and plaice have always
been popular with the chip shops. Ray (or skate), cod,
hake and haddock are all plentiful and moderately priced
fish, just waiting to be appreciated more widely. Restaurants need to be encouraged to serve more of it on
a regular basis, but not smothered in heavy sauces or
overcooked to tasteless dryness as has so often been done

in the past. Is it any wonder that customers have tended to be sceptical of fish dishes? If the professional cooks show the fish product respect, treat it properly, serve it simply letting it speak for itself, imagine how popular it could and would become.

It is quite obvious, when one sees the fantastic quality, that the Irish fishermen take great pride in getting their bountiful catch to the markets in a pristine condition.

They handle the fish with care and respect, icing it properly while on the boats to ensure freshness. One really must appreciate these steps because it does make such a difference to the product.

Nowadays, with the healthy diet consciousness becoming more widespread, people are looking for alternatives to their diet. More people are trying fish now than ever before, and hopefully learning to appreciate its wholesome goodness as well as its flavour. The first simple step to take is finding a reliable and knowledgeable fishmonger. After you've done that, there's no limit to what your taste buds can learn.

WARM SALAD OF FISH AND CHIPS

THIS IS A FAVOURITE QUICK LUNCH DISH. THE CRISPY FISH AND CHIPS ARE A GREAT CONTRAST TO THE SALAD. IF YOU'RE CAREFUL WITH YOUR PRESENTATION, IT CAN ALSO BE A VERY ELEGANT STARTER.

SERVES 4

1 large baking potato

oil for deep-frying

salt and freshly ground white pepper

400g (14oz) monkfish fillets

1 egg, lightly beaten

100g (4oz) plain flour

a few mixed salad leaves

2 tablespoons Vinaigrette Dressing (see p. 177)

FOR THE MUSTARD SAUCE

175ml (6 fl oz) double cream

2 tablespoons whole grain mustard

Peel the potato and slice it into wafer thin slices or matchstick-sized chips. Soak the potato in cold water for about 1 hour to remove excess starch.

Pre-heat the deep-fat fryer (or large pot of oil) to 190°C/375°F when a cube of bread browns in about 40 seconds.

Drain the potato chips and dry them off with a cloth. Fry in the hot oil for about 4 minutes or until they are crisp and golden. Drain on kitchen paper and season with salt. Set aside.

To make the mustard sauce, reserve 2 tablespoons of the cream and bring the remainder to the boil in a small pan. Simmer for about 1 minute until slightly thickened. Remove from the heat and whisk in the mustard.

Slice the monkfish fillets into pieces 1cm ($\frac{1}{2}$in) thick. Whisk together the egg and reserved cream and rub this vigorously into the monkfish pieces. Dredge the monkfish in the flour, pushing the flour into the fish pieces so that all the cream/egg mixture is absorbed.

Fry the monkfish in the hot oil (again at 190°C/375°F) for 3 minutes or until crisp and nicely brown. Remove, place on kitchen paper and season with salt and pepper.

To serve, toss the salad leaves in the vinaigrette and divide between 4 plates. Top the salad leaves with the fish pieces and the chips. Drizzle with the mustard sauce and serve at once.

Skate Meunière with Creamed Potatoes, Red Wine and Capers

IN THIS SIMPLE DISH, EACH INGREDIENT DEPENDS ON THE QUALITY OF THE OTHER FOR THE SUCCESS OF THE DISH. IF YOU CAN'T GET BEAUTIFUL SKATE, DO IT WITH ANOTHER FISH SUCH AS BRILL OR HADDOCK.

SERVES 6

2kg (4lb 8oz) skate wings

75g (3oz) unsalted butter

75g (3oz) carrots, chopped

50g (2oz) onions, chopped

1 garlic clove, chopped

1 bouquet garni

1 tablespoon tomato purée

1 tablespoon plain flour

$\frac{1}{2}$ bottle full-bodied red wine

250ml (8 fl oz) Brown Chicken Stock (see p. 178)

50g (2oz) capers, extra fine

FOR THE CREAMED POTATOES

100ml ($3\frac{1}{2}$fl oz) whipping cream

1 quantity Puréed Potatoes (see recipe for Champ, p. 139)

fresh flat-leaved parsley to garnish

To prepare the skate, fillet and skin the skate wings. This can be a difficult job so perhaps your fishmonger could do it for you. Have him reserve the bones for your sauce but he can discard the skin. Trim the skate fillets into 7.5cm (3in) squares for easy sautéing.

In a large pan, sweat the carrots and onions in 25g (1oz) of the butter until very lightly coloured. Add the skate bones, garlic, bouquet garni, tomato purée and flour and sweat for a further 4 minutes. Add the wine, bring to the boil then boil until the wine has reduced by two-thirds. Add the brown stock, return to the boil and simmer for 20 minutes.

Strain the sauce through a fine sieve into a small pan and boil until reduced to a sauce consistency. Season with salt and pepper then whisk in 1 tablespoon of butter to mellow the sauce.

To make the creamed potatoes, bring the cream to the boil in a pan then add to the puréed potatoes. Stir with a whisk to a very smooth consistency and check for seasoning. Set aside in a warm place.

To fry the skate wings, heat the remaining butter in a large frying-pan over a high heat. When the butter is foamy, add the skate wings and season with salt and pepper. Fry gently for 2 minutes on each side then add the capers. Remove from the heat and allow to sit in the frying-pan while you set up the plates.

To serve, spoon some of the creamed potatoes on to the top end of the warmed plates. Arrange the skate fillets in front of the potatoes, spooning a little of the caper butter juice from the pan on to each piece. Surround with a little of the red wine sauce and garnish with parsley sprigs.

GRILLED DOVER SOLE
WITH HERB BUTTER
AND GRILLED LEEKS

DOVER SOLE HAS TO BE ONE OF THE LUSHEST FISH ABOUT. SERVING IT ON THE BONE LIKE THIS MAY
SEEM LAZY BUT IT REALLY ADDS SO MUCH FLAVOUR AND MOISTURE TO THE DELICATE FLESH.

SERVES 4

4 whole Dover sole, each 500g
(1lb 2oz)

100g (4oz) unsalted butter

4 medium-sized leeks

2 tablespoons light olive oil

FOR THE HERB BUTTER

$\frac{1}{2}$ bottle red wine (if preferred,
use white)

1 shallot, finely chopped

$\frac{1}{2}$ garlic clove, chopped

1 teaspoon salt

$\frac{1}{2}$ teaspoon freshly ground
black pepper

$\frac{1}{2}$ teaspoon chopped fresh
thyme

1 tablespoon chopped fresh
parsley

250g (9oz) unsalted butter,
diced, at room temperature

To make the herb butter, boil the red wine in a small pan with the chopped shallot until the wine has reduced to about 6 tablespoons. Remove from the heat and add the garlic, salt and pepper and herbs. Add the butter and mash or whisk together the red wine infusion without melting the butter (a food processor does the job in half the time). Transfer the butter to a small bowl and keep at room temperature.

To prepare the Dover sole, cut off the heads at a slight angle and discard. Turn the fish dark skin upwards, and with a sharp knife cut across the skin where the tail joins the body. Starting at the cut, use the point of a knife to prise a flap of skin away from the flesh until you can obtain a firm grip on it. Grasp the flap of skin in one hand. With the other, hold down the tail, using a cloth to prevent your fingers from slipping. Firmly and decisively pull the skin

up towards the head and it will pull right off.

Turn the fish over and grip it by the tail and using the edge of a knife or a fish scaler, scrape towards the head to remove the scales from the white skin. It is a good idea to scale the fish in a large basin or in a plastic bag to prevent the scales from being scattered around the kitchen. Rinse the fish under cold running water and pat dry on kitchen paper. This whole process can seem time-consuming but it is good fun. If you don't enjoy this type of thing, have your fishmonger do it for you.

Pre-heat the grill. Heavily butter a baking tray.

Season the sole with salt and pepper and lay the fish skin side up on the tray. Smear the skin with butter and place under the grill. Allow to cook skin side up for about 7 minutes, basting the fish with the cooking juices every minute or so. Pour off and reserve these cooking juices. Add 2 tablespoons of the herb butter. Cover the fish with foil and allow to rest away from the heat while you prepare the leeks.

To prepare the leeks, pull away any wilted or old leaves. Cut in half lengthways and wash under cold running water. Par-boil the leeks for 4 minutes in boiling, salted water. Refresh the leeks in cold water to set the colour, then allow to drain well. Toss the leeks in olive oil and grill them in a pan (or barbecue) for about 3 minutes or until nicely charred and marked.

To serve, carefully lift the fish on to warm plates and garnish each plate with some grilled leeks. Spoon a dollop of herb butter on top of each fish and drizzle each plate with the precious cooking juices from the baking tray.

BAKED HADDOCK WITH COURGETTES, LEMON AND THYME

THIS IS A SIMPLE ONE-PAN DISH THAT CAN BE DONE WITH ANY FISH.

SERVES 4

120g (4½oz) unsalted butter

2 medium courgettes, sliced, or cut into batons

2 shallots, finely chopped

8 firm white mushrooms, sliced

salt and freshly ground white pepper

4 fillets of haddock, weighing about 200g (7oz) each

3 tablespoons lemon juice

½ teaspoon fresh thyme leaves (or ¼ teaspoon dried thyme)

Pre-heat the oven to Gas Mark 7/220°C/425°F.

Heavily butter a ceramic baking dish with one half of the butter. Lay the vegetables in the dish, and season them lightly with salt and pepper. Season the haddock fillets lightly, and lay them on top of the vegetables. Use up the rest of the butter by topping each fillet with a generous piece of it. Sprinkle the fish with the lemon juice and thyme. Cover the dish tightly with aluminium foil, and bake in the oven for 8 minutes.

Serve immediately, spooning some of the vegetables and buttery juices onto each plate with each fillet.

SALT CHILLI TURBOT ON A BED OF WILTED GREENS

Inspired by a classic Chinese culinary technique, we have twisted the recipe so that the chilli appears in the sauce and the salt as crunchy rock salt sprinkled on at the last moment.

SERVES 4

750g (1½lb) turbot fillets, about 1cm (½in) thick

2 garlic cloves, finely chopped

100ml (3½fl oz) virgin olive oil

8 anchovy fillets, finely crushed

2 fresh chillies

8 plum tomatoes, skinned, seeded and roughly chopped

juice of ½ lemon

salt and freshly ground black pepper

50g (2oz) baby spinach leaves

50g (2oz) cos lettuce leaves

50g (2oz) rocket

coarse sea salt

To make the tomato chilli sauce, fry the garlic in a little olive oil for 4 minutes over a moderately low heat until soft. Add the anchovies, chillies and tomatoes. Quickly bring to the boil and simmer for 1 minute. Remove from the heat, allow to cool slightly and then add the remaining the olive oil, a little lemon juice and some salt and pepper to taste. Set aside.

To prepare the turbot, trim the fillets, skinning them if necessary, then divide into 4 equal portions. Set the fillets into a Chinese bamboo steamer basket and season very lightly with salt. Put the basket above the fish to steam for about 5 minutes. The cooking time will vary greatly according to the thickness of the fillets.

To serve, arrange the greens neatly in the middle of 4 warm plates and surround with the tomato chilli sauce. Set the turbot fillets directly on top of the greens so that they will wilt from the heat of the fillets. Finally, sprinkle the turbot fillets with some coarse sea salt.

STEAMED SYMPHONY OF SEAFOOD WITH SAFFRON BUTTER VINAIGRETTE

STEAMING IS A GREAT AND VERY FORGIVING TECHNIQUE FOR COOKING COMPLEX DISHES. THIS DISH IS COMPLEX IN THAT YOU HAVE SO MANY SMALL PIECES OF FISH BUT IT IS A SPECTACULAR DISH AND WORTH TRYING. A SELECTION OF ABOUT SIX TO EIGHT VERY FRESH FISH AND SHELLFISH IS NEEDED; USE WHAT IS AVAILABLE TO YOU. THE FOLLOWING ARE JUST EXAMPLES.

SERVES 4

about 120g (4½oz) each of 6–8 fish or shellfish (salmon, brill, lemon sole, hake, monkfish, haddock, prawns, mussels, scallops)

FOR THE BUTTER VINAIGRETTE

150g (5oz) unsalted butter

150ml (5 fl oz) dry white wine

1 shallot, finely chopped

pinch of saffron threads

150ml (5 fl oz) fish stock

salt and freshly ground white pepper

2 tomatoes, skinned, seeded and chopped

2 sprigs of fresh tarragon, chopped

buttered spinach and potatoes to serve as an accompaniment

Carefully trim the fish fillets, making sure that they are nicely shaped and free of bones. Cut the fillets into appropriate sizes, making sure that you have 4 pieces of each fish being used. Save the trimmings and bones to infuse in the sauce.

To make the butter vinaigrette, clarify the butter by bringing it to simmer in a small pan. Skim off any froth which comes to the surface. When the surface has cleared, let the butter settle and simply pour the butter off, leaving behind any watery, milky liquid. Discard the milky liquid and reserve the butter.

Bring the wine to a simmer in a small pan with the shallot, saffron threads and fish trimmings and simmer until the liquid has reduced to about 3 tablespoons. Add the fish stock and simmer again until you have approx-imately 200–230ml (7–7½ fl oz) remaining. Strain this liquid through a fine sieve. Season with salt and pepper. Add the chopped tomato, tarragon and clarified butter and the vinaigrette is ready.

To steam the fish, butter a large steaming basket and arrange the pieces of fish carefully in it. Season with salt only (pepper at this stage makes the fish look dirty). Place over a pan of boiling water, cover and steam for about 4 minutes until the fish is cooked.

To serve arrange some spinach as a bed for the fish. Arrange the pieces attractively on top of the spinach and spoon over the warm saffron butter vinaigrette. Serve with boiled potatoes.

CHARGRILLED SQUID WITH NOODLES, CHILLI AND CORIANDER

SQUID CAN BE AN ACQUIRED TASTE, BUT WE'VE FOUND THAT OUR CUSTOMERS FIND IT MORE APPROACHABLE COOKED THIS WAY. WHATEVER THE REASON, IT'S DEFINITELY WORTH THE EFFORT.

SERVES 4

450g (1lb) fresh squid

150g (5oz) cellophane noodles

vegetable oil

FOR THE VINAIGRETTE

25g (1oz) fresh ginger root

4 tablespoons wine vinegar

1 tablespoon mushroom soy or dark soy sauce

2 tablespoons chilli sauce

1 bunch fresh coriander, picked and roughly chopped

salt and freshly ground white pepper

175ml (6 fl oz) vegetable oil

120ml (4 fl oz) sesame oil

FOR THE PEPPER GARNISH

175ml (6 fl oz) rice wine vinegar

3 tablespoons sugar

1 red pepper

TO GARNISH

prepared salad greens

sesame seeds, toasted

chopped fresh coriander

To make the vinaigrette, combine all the ingredients except the oils in a bowl and whisk until the salt has dissolved. Slowly whisk in the oils. Adjust the seasoning to taste.

To make the pepper garnish, bring the rice wine vinegar and sugar to the boil in a small pan. Cut the pepper into 4 lengthways and remove the seeds. Cut into fine slices and add to the 'gastric'. Simmer for 10 minutes. Set aside in the liquid.

To prepare the squid, separate the head and tentacles from the body and discard the stiff cartilage quill. Cut the head off just above the eyes and reserve the tentacles. Remove the purplish skin and rinse the meat thoroughly in cold water. Cut the body into 4cm (1½in) pieces. Dredge the squid in a little vegetable oil and season with salt and pepper.

Soak the cellophane noodles for about 15 minutes in warm water and drain. Some cellophane noodles require no cooking if they have been soaked, but depending on the type you have you may need to cook for 1–2 minutes in a pot of boiling salted water. Either way, drain and toss in a little sesame oil. Place a pile in the middle of the plate. Arrange the pepper garnish and salad leaves attractively around the noodles (the noodles are served at room temperature).

Quickly chargrill the squid for about 45 seconds on a very hot grill or barbecue (or in a cast iron pan). Serve immediately with the vinaigrette sprinkled liberally on top and garnished with the sesame seeds and lots of fresh coriander.

7

THE DUCK POND

THERE HAVE PROBABLY always been ducks in Ireland. Farmyards would have had their few along with the chickens, and shooting, a popular sport in the countryside, would have yielded up wild ones. Such a commonly found bird, it is nevertheless often avoided by so many. Surely this must just be out of lack of knowledge or confidence in what to do with it. That is a great shame because it tends to have more flavour than chicken without coming across as too 'gamey' or strong. Perhaps it is the composition of the duck that seems off-putting. Ducks have a large frame, comparatively little meat and a much higher fat content than chicken. However, these qualities do have their benefits. Duck carcases are fantastic for stocks and soups, so full of robust and hearty flavour! The fat can also be used to the cook's advantage. Most importantly, it helps keep the meat moist during cooking. It can be trimmed off, rendered (boiled down) and used as a cooking medium for other products.

Don't think ducks should be saved for holiday meals only. They are relatively inexpensive nowadays and widely available. The simplest (and one of the tastiest) ways to cook a duck is just to roast it whole. Simply

season it with some salt and pepper and put it in a medium hot oven (Gas Mark 4/180°C/350°F) for about 2 hours. Give it a try and you'll wonder why you didn't try it sooner.

Don't forget the possibility of goose, either. Because of its size, it is usually reserved for the bigger family occasions, but most recipes for duck can be applied to geese as well. Duck is one of the most popular dishes in our restaurant which leads us to believe that people really do appreciate it. So try one and enjoy.

The first three recipes in this chapter have been designed to create an elaborate meal using just one duck as the mainstay. You can use the carcass, the giblets, the wings and the duck fillets for the soup, the legs and the fat for the Crispy Duck *Confit* and the breast meat for the Peppered Duck Breast.

DUCK SOUP WITH
CORIANDER DUMPLINGS

CONSOMMÉ CAN SOMETIMES BE A BIT LIGHT FOR THOSE WITH A HEARTY APPETITE.
THE ADDITION OF DUMPLINGS OR NOODLES CAN BE THE PERFECT SOLUTION —
AND IT ALSO ADDS ANOTHER DIMENSION.

SERVES 4

FOR THE STOCK

1 duck carcass, neck and
wings

100g (4oz) onions, chopped

100g (4oz) carrots, chopped

$\frac{1}{2}$ garlic bulb

1 bouquet garni

3 cloves

FOR THE DUMPLINGS

1 duck liver, heart and gizzard

2 inner fillets duck breast

2 rashers fatty bacon

1 small onion, finely chopped

2 slices bread, crusts removed,
soaked in milk and squeezed

1 garlic clove, minced

1 egg, lightly beaten

50g (2oz) plain flour

salt and freshly ground white
pepper

2 tablespoons chopped fresh
coriander

2 leaves lettuce, finely sliced

1 tomato, diced

Put the carcass in a large pot with just enough water to cover. Bring to the boil, skimming away any fat and scum which come to the surface. Add the chopped vegetables, garlic, bouquet garni and cloves and simmer gently for about 2 hours. Strain through a sieve.

Mince the liver, heart, gizzard, inner fillets and the bacon. Add the remaining dumpling ingredients and mix together until just combined. Form them into walnut-sized balls. Poach these dumplings in salted water for 5 minutes.

To serve heat the dumplings in the broth and check for seasoning. Divide the lettuce and tomato between the bowls and then ladle the broth and dumplings over the top.

OVERLEAF

Left: *Crispy Duck Confit with Chinese Spices (page 76)*

Right: *Roast Spiced Duck Breast with Honey and Soy Sauce (page 78)*

CRISPY DUCK CONFIT WITH CHINESE SPICES

The best way to describe the texture of a confit is to compare it to that Chinese favourite, crispy aromatic duck. It simply falls off the bone, moist shreds infused with the flavour of the marinade.

SERVES 4

2 duck legs

2 tablespoons chopped fresh ginger root

1 garlic clove, chopped

1 teaspoon white peppercorns

$\frac{1}{2}$ teaspoon anise powder

4 tablespoons coarse sea salt

fat from the duck carcass

150ml (5 fl oz) water

peanut oil or chicken fat

FOR THE SAUCE

1 tablespoon duck fat

1 shallot, chopped

1 teaspoon chopped fresh ginger root

150ml (5 fl oz) duck stock or water

2 whole star anise

1 teaspoon clear honey

1 teaspoon hoisin sauce

a pinch of chilli flakes

soy sauce to taste

TO GARNISH

$\frac{1}{2}$ cucumber

1 spring onion, finely chopped

Twenty-four hours before using, marinate the duck legs. Place them in a dish and scatter the ingredients evenly over the legs.

Chop the duck fat roughly and place in a pan. Add the water and simmer for about 2 hours or until the fat begins to look clear. Strain the fat into a clean pan ready to cook the duck legs.

Rinse the excess spices off the marinated legs, removing the salt as well. Put the legs into the duck fat (if the fat does not completely cover the legs, top it up with the peanut oil or chicken fat). Simmer the legs very gently for $1\frac{1}{2}$ hours or until they are very tender. Allow to cool in the fat.

To make the sauce, fry the shallots and ginger gently in the duck fat until lightly brown. Add the remaining sauce ingredients. Simmer until the stock has reached a sauce consistency which will coat the back of a spoon. Correct the seasoning with soy sauce and, if needed, salt.

Peel the cucumber. Make nice long ribbons by peeling very heavily with a vegetable peeler.

Pre-heat the grill or oven to Gas Mark 6/200°C/400°F.

To serve, crisp up the duck legs by placing them underneath the hot grill, skin side up (or skin side down in a heavy frying-pan), or in the pre-heated oven for 5 minutes. Arrange the cucumber rib- bons on warm plates. Set the confit legs on top, scatter with the spring onions and surround with a little sauce.

PEPPERED DUCK BREAST WITH SPINACH, MUSHROOMS AND CREAM

PEKIN OR AYLESBURY DUCK BREASTS, WITHOUT THE SKIN, ARE PERFECT FOR FLASH-FRYING.
THEY CAN BE COOKED AS SIMPLY AS ANY STEAK AND LEND THEMSELVES TO ALMOST ANY RECIPE.
HERE WE COULDN'T RESIST DOING THE CLASSIC PEPPER STEAK — DUCK, THAT IS!

SERVES 4

2 duck breasts, skin removed

2 tablespoons black
peppercorns, cracked

salt

3 tablespoons unsalted butter

2 tablespoons vegetable oil

100ml ($3\frac{1}{2}$ fl oz) cognac

100ml ($3\frac{1}{2}$ fl oz) reduced duck
stock

100ml ($3\frac{1}{2}$ fl oz) double or
whipping cream

TO GARNISH

100g (4oz) fresh spinach

2 tablespoons unsalted butter

100g (4oz) button
mushrooms

1 tablespoon vegetable oil

Spread the cracked peppercorns on to the duck breasts pressing down the pepper to encrust the duck breasts. Season the breasts with salt. Heat the butter and oil in a frying-pan and fry the duck breasts gently for 3 minutes on each side for medium rare or 5 minutes each side for well done. Remove the duck breasts from the pan and keep warm. De-glaze the pan with the cognac and a little duck stock, stirring well to scrape up the meat juices. Add the cream and simmer to reduce to the sauce consistency preferred.

Season the spinach with salt and fry in half the butter. Fry the mushrooms in the remaining butter with the oil. Mix the two together.

To serve, spoon the spinach and mushroom mixture on to warmed plates. Slice the duck breasts and arrange on top of the spinach. Surround with the sauce.

ROAST SPICED DUCK BREAST WITH HONEY AND SOY SAUCE

THIS RECIPE GIVES YOU THE CLASSIC RESTAURANT TECHNIQUE FOR COOKING BARBARY DUCK BREASTS.
ONCE PRACTISED, YOU'LL FIND IT SIMPLE AND FOOLPROOF.

SERVES 4

2 large Barbary duck breasts, boneless, about 350g (12oz) each

salt and freshly ground white pepper

cayenne pepper

1 tablespoon chopped fresh ginger root

a pinch of chilli peppers

2 tablespoons clear honey

2 tablespoons mushroom soy sauce

1 tablespoon tomato ketchup

2 tablespoons medium sherry

100ml (4 fl oz) chicken stock

lime juice

Pre-heat the oven to Gas Mark 7/220°C/425°F.

To prepare and cook the duck, trim the duck breasts and lightly score the skin side with a sharp knife. Season the skin with salt, turn the breasts over and season with salt, pepper and a little cayenne pepper.

Place the duck breasts skin side down in a hot, dry oven-proof frying-pan. Let them cook over a moderate heat for about 5 minutes or until the skin is nicely golden and crisp. Pour off any excess fat, turn the breasts over and cook for about 1 minute to seal the other side. Turn them back on to their skin sides and place the pan in the pre-heated oven for about 4 minutes for medium rare, 6 minutes for medium, or 10 minutes for well done. Remove the duck breasts from the pan and let them rest while you make the sauce.

To make the sauce, pour off any fat left in the pan. Add all the other ingredients and boil for 2 minutes to thicken to a sauce consistency which will coat the back of a spoon. Taste the sauce carefully and add a squeeze of lime juice or soy sauce if you feel that it needs it.

To serve, slice the duck breasts thinly and arrange on warm plates. Pour over a little sauce and serve at once.

WARM SALAD OF SAUTÉED DUCK LIVERS WITH SLICED POTATOES AND GREEN BEANS

SOAKING THE LIVERS IN MILK TAKES AWAY ANY UNPLEASANT, BITTER TASTES.
KEEP THEM PINK IN THE MIDDLE SO THEY RETAIN THEIR SILKY TEXTURE.

SERVES 4

500g (1lb 2oz) duck livers

250ml (8 fl oz) milk

150g (5oz) baby salad potatoes

100g (4oz) fine green beans

1 shallot, finely chopped

1 tablespoon hazelnuts, roasted and chopped

salt and freshly ground white pepper

4 tablespoons unsalted butter

FOR THE HAZELNUT VINAIGRETTE

1 teaspoon Dijon mustard

2 tablespoons white wine vinegar

salt and freshly ground white pepper

100ml (4 fl oz) hazelnut oil

50ml (2 fl oz) ground-nut or sunflower oil

To prepare the livers, trim off any sinew and green bile spots. Soak the livers in the milk for at least 2 hours, or overnight if possible.

To make the hazelnut vinaigrette, whisk the mustard, wine vinegar, salt and pepper in a small bowl until the salt has dissolved. Slowly whisk in the oils, whisking constantly. Taste and adjust the seasoning.

To prepare the vegetables, cook the potatoes in their skins in boiling, salted water until tender, then drain and refresh in cold water. Peel off the skin and slice into rounds. Season with salt and pepper. Drizzle with a little of the vinaigrette and keep in a warm place.

Cook the green beans in boiling salted water for about 5 minutes until tender, then drain and refresh in plenty of cold water. Drain and cut into 1cm ($\frac{1}{2}$in) lengths. Season with salt and pepper. Add the chopped shallot, hazelnuts

and a few tablespoons of the hazelnut vinaigrette. Don't add the vinaigrette too early or the beans will lose their bright green colour.

To sauté the livers, take the livers out of the milk and drain them on kitchen paper. Season generously with salt and pepper. Heat the butter in a large frying-pan over high heat until the butter is foaming. Add the livers in one layer and allow them to brown without shaking them, for about 3 minutes. Turn them over and cook for a further 1 minute. The livers should remain slightly pink inside.

To serve, spoon the sliced potatoes on to the centre of warm plates and surround with the green bean mixture. Arrange the livers on top of the potatoes and serve at once.

MARSALA CRÈME BRÛLÉE

DUCK YOLKS DEFINITELY GIVE A CREAMIER RESULT TO THIS SIMPLE DESSERT.
THE SLIGHTLY LOWER RATIO OF EGGS TO MILK AND CREAM ALSO HELPS PREVENT THAT 'EGGINESS'
ALL TOO OFTEN FOUND IN CUSTARDS. JEANNE DOESN'T USUALLY ENJOY CUSTARDS, YET SHE FINDS
THIS ONE ABSOLUTELY LUSH. IT IS DELICIOUS SERVED WITH A BISCUIT ON THE SIDE, A SHORTBREAD
OF SOME SORT IS OUR FAVOURITE (SEE P. 186).

SERVES 4–6

350ml (12 fl oz) milk

350ml (12 fl oz) whipping or single cream

$\frac{1}{4}$ vanilla pod, split

100g (4oz) caster sugar

3 tablespoons water

5 duck egg yolks

1 whole duck egg

2 tablespoons Marsala (optional)

50g (2oz) granulated sugar

Pre-heat the oven to Gas Mark 2/150°C/300°F.

Put the milk, cream and vanilla pod in a pan and bring to the boil. Set aside to let the vanilla infuse.

Place half the caster sugar in a small heavy-based pan with the water. Boil until the mixture turns to a light golden caramel, occasionally brushing down the sides of the pan with a pastry brush dipped in water to ensure it doesn't crystallize. Remove from the heat and carefully pour the caramel into the milk mixture. Then return it to a low heat for a couple of minutes, just to let the caramel dissolve.

Whisk the egg yolks, egg and remaining caster sugar together until it is light and pale and the sugar has dissolved. Whisking this mixture continually, slowly pour in the milk mixture and whisk until thoroughly blended. Add the Marsala, if using, then strain through a fine conical sieve.

Pour the mixture evenly into ovenproof serving bowls and place them in a roasting tin filled with hot water to come half-way up the sides of the bowls. Cover this completely with cling film to prevent a crust from forming on the pots while cooking. Place in the pre-heated oven and cook for about 30 minutes until set. The mixture should still wobble slightly if you shake the dish.

Remove from the oven, remove the cling film and leave to cool in the bain-marie. Place in the fridge.

To brûlée the top, sprinkle a thin, even layer of granulated sugar over the top of the chilled custards and then place under a hot grill until evenly caramelized. Alternatively, a blow torch can be used for this. The sugar will melt then harden to a crisp, golden caramel.

8

THE GAME LARDER

GAME, SUCH A simple word and yet think of the romantic images it conjures up. Grand hunts on stately great estates, aristocratic gentry dressed in splendid style, crisp chilly mornings, vibrant autumn colours, a great tradition from another era. But game is no longer the privilege of the upper classes. In fact, it is widely available here in Ireland since there is so much of it being farmed. One can actually enjoy venison, rabbit, quail, partridge and pheasant without being at all involved in sport.

Nearly all the various types of farms raise their stocks sympathetically. That is, the animals or birds feed on natural foods and live in natural or near natural sur-roundings, therefore producing a totally organic product as a result. This is great for the public image especially when one hears all the scary reports of the drugs and chemicals that are so widespread in other livestock rearing. Most game is remarkably lean; venison in fact has lower fat and cholesterol count than any other red meat, making it a very viable health alternative.

All game does need to be hung, usually anywhere between several days and just over a week. This does two important things. It tenderizes the meat and it also develops the flavour, although, of course, there are endless debates about the merits of shorter or longer hanging times and so on. Older, tougher animals will also benefit from being marinated before cooking, as this also helps to tenderize the meat.

Because of its leanness, game is almost always wrapped or larded with fat to ensure that it doesn't have a chance to dry out during the cooking process. It is not always necessary though. A careful eye, frequent bastings and shorter cooking times can also overcome the dryness.

Game of delicate flavour, quail or partridge for example, do best when prepared simply. Plainly roast or grilled, the fine qualities can speak for themselves. Traditionally, large game is matched with rich ingredients. The robust flavours can carry wine, spirits, cream and spices. Often the richness of the meat is offset by the light tartness of a fruit: orange or kumquat sauce, redcurrant or cranberry jelly, compote of plums, cherries, apricots or grapes to suggest but a few. Many game recipes are interchangeable as long as you bear in mind that the length of cooking times would need to be adjusted.

Most butchers and many supermarkets are now reliable sources of game. Venison distributed by the Irish Deer Farmers' Association is quality controlled. Rabbit can frequently be seen sitting beside the chickens on the shelf, as can quail, pheasant and other game. The wonderful thing is they are remarkably reasonable in price. It's time the old image of game as expensive and exclusive went out the window.

LOIN OF HARE WITH BACON AND IRISH WHISKEY CREAM

HARE IS A FOOD WHICH MOST PEOPLE JUST DON'T FANCY. YET TO US, IT'S ONE OF THE TASTIEST AND BEST VALUE ITEMS AROUND. INTRODUCE YOURSELF TO IT BY TRYING IT AT YOUR MOST TRUSTED RESTAURANT OR JUST TRY THIS RECIPE. BUSHMILL'S IS THE BEST WHISKEY TO USE IF YOU CAN BUY IT.

SERVES 6

550g (1¼lb) boneless hare loin, well trimmed

12 rashers streaky bacon

1 tablespoon vegetable oil

1 tablespoon unsalted butter

FOR THE SPICE MIXTURE

6 juniper berries

2 whole cloves

¼ teaspoon dried thyme

½ teaspoon whole black peppercorns

½ teaspoon salt

FOR THE SAUCE

250ml (8 fl oz) Brown Chicken Stock (see p. 178)

120ml (4 fl oz) double cream

5 tablespoons Irish whiskey

Grind the spices together in a mortar and pestle or a small coffee grinder.

Slice the hare loin into 12 even-sized medallions and sprinkle the meat evenly with the spice mixture. Drizzle 2 tablespoons of whiskey over them. Wrap each medallion with a slice of bacon around its circumference and fix it in place with a cocktail stick.

Fry the medallions over high heat in a heavy-based frying-pan with oil and butter for about 3 minutes on each side. Pour the remaining whiskey into the pan and ignite it to flambé the hare. Remove the meat and allow it to rest in a warm place while finishing the sauce. Add the cream and the stock to the pan and boil over high heat until a sauce consistency is achieved.

Place 2 medallions on each of the warm plates and pour the sauce around. Serve with something like the roast vegetables on pages 128–9.

STUFFED QUAIL WITH BUTTERED RISOTTO

WE FIND THAT QUAIL IS THE MOST APPROACHABLE OF ALL GAME BIRDS. IT'S FORGIVING TO COOK AND IT LENDS ITSELF TO ALL SORTS OF RECIPES. THIS ONE IS NICE BECAUSE YOU DON'T HAVE TO MESS ABOUT WITH BONES. ASK YOUR BUTCHER TO BONE THE QUAIL AS IT IS A FIDDLY JOB.

SERVES 4

8 boneless quail

FOR THE RISOTTO

90g (3½oz) unsalted butter

1 small onion, finely chopped

150g (5oz) Arborio rice

700ml (23½fl oz) chicken stock,

salt and freshly ground black pepper

FOR THE STUFFING

165g (5½oz) fresh spinach

1 shallot, chopped

1 garlic clove, chopped

25g (1oz) bacon, diced

15g (½oz), dried ceps, soaked for 15 minutes and diced

65g (2½oz) unsalted butter

120g (4½oz) chicken livers

1 tablespoon pine nuts, toasted

TO GARNISH

a few sprigs of fresh rosemary or thyme

Pre-heat the oven to Gas Mark 6/200°C/400°F. Butter a roasting tin.

To make the risotto, melt one-third of the butter in a heavy-based pan and fry the onion over medium heat until soft and transparent. Add the rice and then the chicken stock, a ladle full at a time, stirring frequently for about 20 minutes until the rice is almost cooked. Season to taste. Set aside in a warm place.

Meanwhile make the stuffing. Blanch the spinach with a little water over a high heat for 1–2 minutes until soft then drain and squeeze out any excess water. Fry the shallot, garlic, bacon and ceps in the butter over medium heat in a large frying-pan. Add the chicken livers and pine nuts and cook for a few minutes until they are just softened and browned. Chop this mixture up roughly. Add the spinach and mix together thoroughly. Taste for seasoning and adjust if necessary.

Stuff each quail with one-eighth of the mixture, sealing them closed by pulling the skin over the opening. Place in the buttered roasting tin.

Roast in the pre-heated oven for 10–15 minutes. Because the bird is so small and the filling is already cooked and warm, it should not take any longer.

To serve, stir the remaining butter into the warm risotto and place 1–2 spoonfuls in the centre of each of the warm plates to make a bed for the quails. Place 2 birds on each plate and garnish with a sprig of herbs, if desired. Serve immediately.

ROAST PARTRIDGE WITH BACON, GARLIC AND THYME

THIS IS A GREAT RECIPE FOR MOST GAME BIRDS. TRY IT WITH PIGEON, PHEASANT OR GROUSE.

SERVES 2

2 young partridge, drawn, livers reserved

salt and freshly ground black pepper

10 garlic cloves, blanched for 10 minutes

4 sprigs of fresh thyme

6 rashers streaky bacon

2 tablespoons light olive oil

100g (4oz) unsalted butter

2 shallots, sliced

250ml (8 fl oz) Brown Chicken Stock (see p. 178)

Pre-heat the oven to Gas Mark 7/220°C/425°F.

Season the birds inside and out with salt and pepper and stuff the garlic and a sprig of fresh thyme inside each bird. Drape the bacon slices over each bird and truss into place with string.

Heat the oil and 1 tablespoon of butter in a large ovenproof pan until the butter is foaming and very hot. Add the partridge and fry briefly on all sides. Turn the birds on to their sides, place in the pre-heated oven and roast for 8–10 minutes on each side. Remove from the oven, turn the birds breast down and allow the birds to rest for 5 minutes. Remove from the pan.

Using the same pan that the partridge were cooked in, sweat the shallots in a little butter. Meanwhile, untie the birds and remove the bacon and the garlic cloves. Chop the bacon into 5mm ($\frac{1}{4}$in) pieces. Set aside with the cloves.

Cut off the legs and the breasts from the birds and keep in a warm place. Chop the carcase and livers and add to the shallots. Cook gently for a few minutes. Add the stock, thyme and 2 garlic cloves. Simmer for 5 minutes then strain through a fine sieve into a small pan. Boil until reduced to a sauce consistency which coats the back of a spoon. Whisk in a tablespoon of butter and season with salt and pepper and a few leaves of fresh thyme.

To serve, fry the reserved bacon pieces and garlic cloves gently in butter until the bacon is starting to crisp up and the garlic is beginning to brown. Make sure the partridge is still warm and then arrange on warm serving plates. Pour over a little sauce and then garnish with the fried garlic and bacon pieces.

OVERLEAF

Left: *Roast Partridge with Bacon, Garlic and Thyme*

Right: *Warm Game Tart with Roast Winter Vegetables and Green Peppercorns (page 88)*

WARM GAME TART WITH ROAST WINTER VEGETABLES AND GREEN PEPPERCORNS

WE'VE ALWAYS LOVED A GAME TART. IN FACT WE COULD TACKLE ONE NEARLY ANY WINTERY EVENING. USE A SELECTION OF SUITABLE GAME AND A GOOD QUALITY SAUSAGE MEAT FROM YOUR BUTCHER. YOU CAN CHOOSE WHICHEVER VEGETABLES YOU LIKE OR HAVE TO HAND. GOOD QUALITY PUFF PASTRY IS AVAILABLE IN MOST DELICATESSENS AND SUPERMARKETS BUT IF YOU CAN MAKE YOUR OWN, ALL THE BETTER.

SERVES 6

FOR THE FILLING

350g (12oz) game meat, well trimmed (pheasant legs, venison shoulder, hare, pigeon, etc.)

150g (5oz) pork sausage meat

75g (3oz) streaky bacon

75g (3oz) back fat

1 tablespoon brandy

1 shallot, chopped

1 garlic clove, chopped

1 tablespoon chopped fresh parsley

1 tablespoon chopped fresh thyme or $\frac{1}{2}$ teaspoon dried thyme

1 teaspoon freshly ground black pepper

$\frac{1}{2}$ teaspoon salt

FOR THE SAUCE

150ml (5 fl oz) double cream

150ml (5 fl oz) meat gravy or stock

2 tablespoons whiskey or cognac

1 tablespoon green peppercorns, lightly crushed

salt

FOR THE VEGETABLES

900g (2lb) mixed vegetables (carrots, potatoes, Brussels sprouts, mushrooms, baby onions, etc.)

120g ($4\frac{1}{2}$oz) unsalted butter

salt and freshly ground black pepper

200g (7oz) Puff Pastry (see p. 182–3), home-made or bought

1 egg yolk, lightly beaten

To make the filling, check that all the game is well trimmed, that it has no 'off' bits or tough sinews. Slice all the meat and fat into manageable pieces about 2.5 × 7.5cm (1 × 3in). Combine all the filling ingredients together in a bowl and mix them roughly! Put the mixture through the coarse blade of your mincer or chop very finely by hand. Beat well with a wooden spoon or by hand, to ensure that it is blended thoroughly. Form into a ball, wrap in cling film and place in the fridge.

On a floured surface, roll out the puff pastry into 2 × 30cm (12in) squares, no thicker than 3mm ($\frac{1}{8}$in). Chill these 2 sheets for at least 20 minutes.

When they are nice and cold, bring out one piece and cut into a large circle about 24cm ($9\frac{1}{2}$in) in diameter. The easiest way to accomplish this is to use an overturned bowl or plate as a guide. Brush this base completely with the egg yolk wash, taking care not to let it drip over the sides.

Place the filling in the centre of the base and with your hands, pat into an even dome shape. There should be a perimeter of at least 4–6cm ($1\frac{1}{2}$–$2\frac{1}{2}$in) of puff pastry all the way around the filling.

Take the other piece of puff from the fridge and quickly reapply egg wash to the perimeter of the base before carefully laying the second piece on top. Carefully, with your hands, gently pat this piece in place, shaping the puff pastry over the filling and sealing the two edges of puff together. Try not to let there be any big air pockets inside and try not to stretch the top piece of puff or it will lose shape during cooking.

Brush the whole top of the tart with the egg yolk wash, making sure not to let it drip over the edges, and cut the edges so that they are even with each other. Pierce a small hole in the centre of the top to let the steam be released during cooking, and decorate with the egg yolk wash as you like. You can achieve this using the back of a knife, the tines of a fork or even a cock-tail stick. Put to chill again in the fridge for 20 minutes.

Pre-heat the oven to Gas Mark4/180°C/350°F.

Bake the tart in the pre-heated oven for about 30 minutes, until golden brown.

To make the sauce, simply boil the cream with the meat stock or gravy until it has thickened to sauce consistency. Add the whiskey or cognac and the green peppercorns (lightly crushing them helps them release their flavour and aroma). Simmer again over low heat for 1–2 minutes and then check for seasoning. Add salt as needed. Keep warm.

To prepare the vegetables, boil or steam the vegetables which you have chosen until they are just cooked. Allow them to cool slightly.

Heat the butter in a large casserole until it is foamy and is just turning brown. Throw all the vegetables in at once and allow them to cook gently in the butter for about 5 minutes. Turn them gently from time to time to ensure that they are all coated with the butter and season with salt and pepper.

To serve, present the tart at the table as a whole, with the vegetables either surrounding it on the plate or on the side in their own serving bowl. Someone can then cut the tart into individual portions, plate it, serve the vegetables and pass the sauce so that each may take as much or little as preferred.

PEPPERED LEG OF VENISON WITH HOT AND SOUR CABBAGE

A WELL HUNG HAUNCH OF YOUNG VENISON IS AT LEAST AS NICE TO EAT AS THE LOIN OR FILLET.
THE TECHNIQUE HERE FOR SEPARATING THE LEG MUSCLES MEANS THAT YOU'RE LEFT WITH SINEW-
FREE 'LOIN' FROM THE LEG.

SERVES 6

1 haunch of venison, about
2½kg (5½lb)

salt and cracked black pepper

2 tablespoons unsalted butter

1 tablespoon vegetable oil

FOR THE SAUCE

50ml (2 fl oz) sherry vinegar

50ml (2 fl oz) meat stock or
gravy (optional)

300ml (10 fl oz) double cream

salt and freshly ground black
pepper

FOR THE HOT AND SOUR
CABBAGE

2 tablespoons unsalted butter

1 red cabbage, finely sliced

50ml (2 fl oz) sherry vinegar

2 eating apples, peeled, cored
and chopped

2 tablespoons raisins

1 tablespoon chopped fresh
ginger root

2 tablespoons sugar

salt and ½ teaspoon freshly
ground white pepper

Pre-heat the oven to Gas Mark 5/190°C/375°F.

To cook the cabbage, melt the butter in a large, heavy-based casserole. Add the cabbage, sherry vinegar and salt. Cover and cook over a low heat for about 1 hour.

Stir in the apples, raisins, ginger and sugar and cook gently for another 30 minutes. Finally, add the white pepper and check the seasoning to see if it needs more sugar or salt.

Meanwhile cook the venison and sauce. Trim the outside of the haunch to remove any sinew and fat. Work carefully to see that you don't remove too much. Separate each large muscle, one at a time and place them to one side. Reserve the trim, shin and very small muscles for another use. Roll the large muscles in cracked black pepper and season them with salt.

Heat a large ovenproof frying-pan and fry the pieces of venison in the butter and oil until they have a nice colour on all sides. Place them in the pre-heated oven for 5 minutes for medium rare or 8 minutes for medium to well done.

Remove the venison pieces from the pan and allow them to rest in a warm place. Pour off any fat from the pan and add the sherry vinegar. Scrape the bottom of the pan with a wooden spoon to loosen all the delicious, caramelized juices. Reduce the sherry vinegar to 1 tablespoon then add the meat gravy, if using, and the cream. Reduce by boiling it quickly until it has reached a sauce consistency. Season with salt and pepper.

To serve, spoon some piping hot cabbage on to warmed plates, slice the venison pieces and arrange the slices neatly on top of the cabbage. Pour over a little sauce and it's ready to serve.

EMINCÉ OF PHEASANT WITH A WILD MUSHROOM CREAM

THE BIGGEST PROBLEM WITH PHEASANT IS ITS TENDENCY TO COOK OUT VERY DRY.
THIS SIMPLE RECIPE GIVES YOU LOADS OF CONTROL TO PREVENT THIS FROM HAPPENING.
IT CAN ALSO BE DONE WITH CHICKEN, GUINEA FOWL OR RABBIT.

SERVES 4

25g (1oz) dried morel mushrooms

4 pheasant breasts, skinned and boned

5 tablespoons unsalted butter

salt and freshly ground black pepper

2 shallots, finely chopped

100ml (3½ fl oz) dry white wine

50ml (2 fl oz) Madeira

250ml (8 fl oz) double cream

100ml (3½ fl oz) chicken stock (optional)

salt and freshly ground white pepper

sautéed buttered Savoy cabbage to garnish

Soak the dried morels in warm water for 30 minutes. Remove them and check that the stalks are free of dirt. Slice the larger ones in half and leave the small ones whole.

Take the pheasant breasts and remove the inside fillet from each one. Push the breast firmly on to a cutting board and slice at an acute angle into 4 escalopes. You now have 5 pieces including the fillet, which makes 1 portion. Repeat this process with the other 3 breasts.

Heat 4 tablespoons of butter in a large sauté pan until it starts to foam then add the pheasant pieces in one layer. Cook gently for 45 seconds on each side then transfer all the pieces from the pan to a plate.

Melt the remaining butter and fry the shallots until soft and transparent. Add the wine, Madeira and morels and cook gently until most of the liquid has evaporated. Add the cream and chicken stock and season with salt and pepper. Simmer gently for about 5 minutes until it has reached a sauce consistency.

Fry some blanched cabbage leaves in a pan with plenty of butter, salt and pepper. Arrange a little of the cabbage on each warm plate. Bring the sauce to the boil, then add the pheasant pieces. Let the sauce come slowly up to a simmer then spoon 5 pheasant pieces and plenty of the sauce on to each plate.

CHAPTER

9

THE PASTURES

I RELAND DOES SEEM like the perfect place to raise cows and sheep. Its superb pastures are lush and green, there's pure air, abundant rainfall and fresh winds to keep them just so. It is a stress-free, disease-free environment, unpolluted, unravaged by modern industry, and it is obvious that it is these factors that contribute to Ireland producing some of the finest beef and lamb, exported all over Europe and to places further afield.

There was always some pork available in Ireland as every farmyard had pigs and would usually slaughter at least one a year, but it used to be that cattle were just kept for dairy produce. It was only when an animal was old and rendered useless that it would be butchered. However, even then the realization that beef was rich and generous in flavour was reached, and when the great estates of the English brought on the huge herds of cattle, it gained in popularity and quickly became established as the traditional highlight of festive days.

Various forms of preservation had to be developed, for only a certain amount could be used up fresh. There is, as a result, a great tradition of salting and curing, all guaranteed to keep the supply of meat throughout the year.

Those large Irish households have a reputation for hearty appetites and it took a careful cook to extend a modest cut into a wholesome meal. The cleverness came through the use of grains and pulses and, of course, those basic vegetables, creating big soups and stews that would fill up even the most hungry of souls.

Lamb stew is probably Ireland's national dish with every housewife having the best recipe around, but really it is a big juicy steak that is still said to be the favourite

by far. Many a man still looks forward to his Saturday night plate of a choice cut of beef.

Today, many of the old-fashioned dishes are creeping back into popularity. Spiced beef, slow braises, whole roasting of joints married naturally to carrots and barley, corned beef and cabbage, these dishes can be found on even upmarket menus. Is this just a trend following the resurgence of regional dishes? Or perhaps people have simply come to their senses and are ready for wholesome, savoury food again.

GRILLED LAMB SHANK WITH BRAISED FENNEL AND GARLIC

LAMB SHANKS HAVE BEEN ENJOYING A POPULAR REVIVAL WORLD-WIDE.
IT IS ABOUT TIME; WE'VE BEEN ENJOYING THESE SUCCULENT PIECES SINCE CHILDHOOD!
THEY'RE AN ITEM NOT TO BE AFRAID OF SINCE THEY ARE REALLY VERY EASY AND FORGIVING TO COOK.

SERVES 4

4 lamb shanks

2 fennel bulbs

2 garlic bulbs

350ml (12 fl oz) water

1 tablespoon black pepper

Pre-heat the oven to Gas Mark $\frac{1}{2}$/120°C/250°F.

Trim the shanks of excess fat and saw off the knuckle. Trim and cut the fennel bulbs in half. Blanch the garlic bulbs in boiling salted water for 5 minutes then remove from heat. When they are cool enough to handle, peel each clove.

Sauté the shanks in a large heavy casserole until nice and brown on all sides. Add 120ml (4 fl oz) of water and pepper. Cover and place in the pre-heated oven for 1 hour. After 1 hour, turn the shanks and add the garlic cloves. After another 30 minutes, add the fennel bulbs and cook for about another 30 minutes. Finally add the black pepper.

Remove from the oven and strain off the juices. Add to these juices the remaining water and simmer over a low heat. Skim off the fat as it comes to the surface. When the sauce is free and clear, strain back over the lamb shanks and serve with the garlic and fennel. This dish goes extremely well with Champ (see p. 139).

LAMBS' LIVER AND SWEETBREADS WITH CRISPY FRIED ONIONS AND LENTILS

THIS IS A RECIPE FOR CONVERTING FOLK WHO DON'T NORMALLY EAT OFFAL. FAMILIAR YET ZINGY, TASTY FLAVOURS SEDUCE THEM – THEN THEY ARE HOOKED! IT CAN BE DONE WITH JUST LIVER OR SWEETBREADS. IT'S NICE AND CHEAP TOO!

SERVES 4

1 large onion

plain flour for dredging

450g (1lb) lamb sweetbreads

salt and freshly ground black pepper

2 tablespoons unsalted butter or oil for frying

750g (1½lb) lambs' liver, sliced 1cm (½in) thick

FOR THE LENTILS

225g (8oz) green or brown lentils

600ml (1 pint) water

2 tablespoons finely chopped onion

1 tablespoon finely chopped carrot

1 tablespoon finely chopped leek

1 bay leaf

a pinch of dried thyme

1 teaspoon salt

120ml (4 fl oz) Vinaigrette Dressing (see p. 177)

To prepare the lentils, wash them and put them in a pan with the water. Bring to the boil and simmer for 5 minutes, skimming the scum which comes to the surface. Add the chopped vegetables, the bay leaf, thyme and salt. Simmer for 20 minutes then leave to cool to lukewarm. Stir in the vinaigrette.

To prepare the onion, slice the large onion into very thin slices against the grain. Dredge lightly in flour and deep-fry in hot oil for about 3 minutes or until crisp and golden. Drain on kitchen paper, season lightly with salt and keep in a warm place.

To cook the liver and sweetbreads, put the sweetbreads in a pan with plenty of cold water. Bring to the boil and simmer gently for 5 minutes. Drain the sweetbreads and refresh them in cold water. Peel off any tough membranous tissue and meat which is attached to the sweetbread. Slice each sweetbread in half lengthways. Set aside. Season the pieces with salt and pepper and sauté the sweetbreads in a mixture of oil and butter. When they are brown and slightly crisp, remove from the pan and keep warm.

Wipe the pan and add some fresh oil and butter. Season the liver and then dredge lightly in flour. Cook the liver on each side for about 2 minutes for pink, or 3 minutes each side for well done.

To serve, spoon the lentils on to warm plates and heap a pile of the crisp onions at the base. Carefully present the liver and sweetbreads on the top of the lentils.

NOISETTES OF LAMB WITH A HERB AND OLIVE CRUST

THIS TECHNIQUE CAN BE APPLIED TO FISH FILLETS JUST AS EASILY AS MEAT. IF YOU WANT TO MAKE IT A LITTLE SIMPLER, LEAVE OUT THE CHICKEN MOUSSE AND SIMPLY BRUSH THE LAMB WITH OLIVE TAPENADE OR MUSTARD AND THEN PRESS ON THE BREADCRUMBS.

SERVES 4

1 saddle of lamb

2 tablespoons light olive oil

1 cup finely chopped carrots, onions and leeks

1 litre (1¾ pints) Brown Chicken Stock (see p. 178)

1 breast of chicken

1 egg white

250ml (8 fl oz) double cream

1 tablespoon chopped fresh parsley

1 tablespoon chopped fresh rosemary

1 tablespoon chopped fresh thyme

65g (2½oz) black olives, stoned and finely chopped

1 garlic clove, finely chopped

50g (2oz) coarse breadcrumbs

2 tablespoons butter

Bone out the saddle of lamb so that you have 2 boneless loins. Cut each loin into 6 pieces. Lightly bat out each noisette with a heavy cleaver. Heat 2 tablespoons of oil in a heavy pan until smoking. Fry each noisette quickly on both sides so that they have a beautiful rich brown colour. Allow to cool.

Chop the lamb bones roughly and brown them off in a heavy pan with the carrots, onions and leeks. Add the chicken stock and simmer for about 1 hour. Strain then return to the pan and boil to reduce to a sauce consistency.

Pre-heat the oven to Gas Mark 6/200°C/400°F.

Purée the chicken breast and egg white in a food processor until smooth. Add the cream in a slow, steady stream and process until you have a smooth homogenous mixture. Add the herbs, olives and garlic and mix these in thoroughly. Spread each noisette with some of the mousse and olive mixture and dip into coarse breadcrumbs, only on the side with the mousse mixture. Place the noisettes in a buttered pan, crusty mousse side up, and put into the pre-heated oven for 4 minutes, then turn each noisette upside down for a further minute. Serve with a little of the lamb sauce and some potatoes and vegetables of your choice.

IRISH STEW

Why is it that Irish stew is so famous? Surely every country has in
its history a basic one-pot dish. Maybe it is just too tasty and wholesome to pass up.
At any rate, this is our current favourite.

SERVES 4

900g (2lb) boneless shoulder
or neck of lamb

1.2 litres (2 pints) water

salt

225g (8oz) potatoes, peeled
and cut into coarse chunks

225g (8oz) carrots, thickly
sliced

225g (8oz) leeks, thickly
sliced

225g (8oz) baby onions,
peeled

2 sprigs of fresh thyme

1 cup of fresh parsley leaves,
blanched

250ml (8 fl oz) double cream

1 tablespoon unsalted butter

Trim and cube the lamb meat. Discard the fatty film and place the lamb into a heavy casserole with the water and a little salt. Bring to the boil then skim off the surface of scum and fat and simmer for 30 minutes.

Add half of the potatoes. Simmer for another 30 minutes then stir up the pot quite vigorously to break up the potatoes. Add the rest of the vegetables and the thyme. Simmer for about another 30 minutes or until the meat and vegetables are all tender. Add the parsley, cream and butter. Re-heat quickly and serve.

OVERLEAF

Left: *Carpaccio of Beef with Roast Aubergines and Balsamic Vinegar (page 100)*

Right: *Irish Stew*

CARPACCIO OF BEEF WITH ROAST AUBERGINES AND BALSAMIC VINEGAR

WITH IRELAND'S PURE AND DISEASE-FREE ENVIRONMENT, THERE IS NO BETTER PLACE TO EAT RAW BEEF. TRY THIS VERSION OF A WORLD FAMOUS CLASSIC DISH, NAMED AFTER A VENETIAN RENAISSANCE PAINTER.

SERVES 4

2 small aubergines

8 garlic cloves

8 tablespoons light olive oil

275g (10oz) fillet of beef

2 tablespoons coarse sea salt

1 teaspoon black peppercorns, cracked

8 tablespoons balsamic vinegar

a few salad leaves to garnish

$\frac{1}{2}$ cup shaved Parmesan

Cut each aubergine into 4 thick slices and gently crush the garlic cloves in their skins. Heat the light olive oil in a heavy-based frying-pan and roast the aubergines and garlic together for 5 minutes on each side. Allow to cool.

Thinly slice the fillet of beef into 8 pieces. Gently pound the slices between 2 pieces of oiled cling film until very thin. Try to have the beef an even thickness. Arrange these slices carefully on 4 plates.

To serve, sprinkle the beef with the sea salt and black peppercorns. Drizzle the beef slices with the balsamic vinegar. Carefully arrange the aubergines, garlic and some salad leaves attractively around the beef. Sprinkle the shaved Parmesan over all of these and top with a little of the olive oil. Serve with crusty country bread.

SAUTÉED FILLET OF BEEF WITH BRAISED OXTAIL, POMME PURÉE AND RED WINE SAUCE

A RICH MAN, POOR MAN TYPE OF DISH, THERE IS NO DOUBT IN OUR MINDS THAT THE POOR OLD OXTAIL ELEVATES THIS DISH A NOTCH OR TWO. TRY THE OXTAIL ON ITS OWN WITH PASTA OR MASHED POTATOES.

SERVES 4

500g (1lb 2oz) oxtail

salt and freshly ground black pepper

50g (2oz) unsalted butter

50g (2oz) shallots, finely chopped

25g (1oz) carrots, finely chopped

25g (1oz) celery, finely chopped

25g (1oz) mushrooms

750ml (1¼ pints) red wine

500ml (17 fl oz) meat stock

1 bouquet garni

4 × 175g (6oz) fillet of beef, trimmed

500g (1lb 2oz) Pomme Purée (see recipe for Champ, p. 139)

TO GARNISH

2 spring onions, trimmed and sliced into fine rings

Pre-heat the oven to Gas Mark 4/180°C/350°F.

Trim the oxtail of all sinew and fat. Cut into segments and season with salt and pepper. Colour the oxtail in half the butter, in a braising pan, until nice and brown all over. Add the shallots, carrots, celery and mushrooms, colour lightly and then add the red wine and boil to reduce by half. Add the meat stock and bouquet garni and bring back to the boil. Skim off the scum. Cover and braise in the pre-heated oven for 2 hours. Remove the oxtail and flake the meat. Set aside in a warm place. Skim the stock and pass through a fine sieve.

Fry the beef fillets gently in a heavy pan with the remaining butter for 3 minutes each side. This depends on the size and shape of the fillets and how you prefer your meat. Set aside on a wire rack to rest for several minutes.

To assemble, place the pomme purée in the centre of warm plates. Place the fillets on top. Carefully place the flaked oxtail over the beef, sprinkle on the sliced spring onions. Spoon the seasoned sauce around the pomme purée.

HOT SMOKED FILLET OF BEEF WITH ROCKET, PINE NUTS AND ROASTED PEPPERS

THIS IS AN INTERESTING TECHNIQUE TO KNOW. IT IS A LITTLE FIDDLY, BUT FUN. IT JUST REQUIRES A LITTLE PRACTICE. IDEALLY A HOME-SMOKER IS THE TICKET, BUT UNFORTUNATELY MANY OF US DO NOT HAVE ONE. YOU NEED TO HAVE A COVERED 'WEBER-STYLE' BARBECUE TO DO THIS RECIPE.

SERVES 4

750g (1lb 10oz) whole beef fillet, trimmed of fat and sinew

salt and black peppercorns, cracked

250g (9oz) rocket leaves

120ml (4 fl oz) Vinaigrette Dressing (see p. 177)

65g (2½oz) pine nuts, toasted

FOR THE ROAST PEPPERS

1 red pepper

1 yellow pepper

3 tablespoons light olive oil

To prepare the barbecue, build a small mound of charcoal in the charcoal pan of the barbecue. Very carefully light the fire. When the coals are covered with white ash they will be very hot and ready for cooking.

When the barbecue is at this stage, brush the peppers with a little oil and grill them for about 10 minutes until the skins are blistered and blackened, turning them frequently to ensure even cooking. Remove them from the heat and when they are cool enough, peel off the skins, halve and seed the peppers and cut into slices. Set aside.

Lay some water-soaked wood such as oak, applewood or hickory on the top of the coals. Season the beef fillet generously with salt and peppercorns and place on the centre of the grill rack. Place on the lid of the barbecue and let the meat cook and sim-ultaneously smoke for about 45 minutes for rare beef, 1½ hours for well done. Watch that the ashes are not too hot in the middle of the rack. If the fire is burning too quickly, slow this down by sprinkling a little water over it.

To serve, dress the rocket with vinaigrette and pile neatly at the top of warm plates. Slice the beef fillet, arrange below the salad and sprinkle with pine nuts. Finally, place a few slices of peppers at the bottom.

CHAPTER

10
THE FOREST

THE ISLE OF Ireland was once a huge forest; mind
you that was a very long time ago. However, one
can see how the damp climate is conducive to
both the forests and their undergrowth. Nowadays, the
hedgerows and wood margins, as well as the many forest
parks, still offer up an overwhelming variety of wild food.

It is a shame that so much of it lies unused due to our
general ignorance. Just what is out there? The native
berries are perhaps the most obvious titbits that one
would encounter if out on a forest hike. Over the summer
months there are wild strawberries and wild cherries. As
summer draws to an end, blackberries and bilberries are
in great profusion. On the old Irish calendar, 'Fraughan
Sunday' was a day specially set aside for going out and
picking the fraughan (bilberries). As autumn
approaches, it is elderberries and rowanberries. The
variety simply puts our cooks' heads spinning.

The variety and quantity of wild mushrooms is beginning to draw more interest again as well. There are cèpes,
chanterelles and hedgehogs to name but a few. Remember
though, if in doubt of a mushroom's identity, don't eat it.
There are courses available on mushroom picking, and
the National Trust offers organized walks.

Then there is the wild sorrel and nettles, popular since early Christian times. There is gorse and coltsfoot – did you even know that they were edible? – camomile, wild marjoram, mint, juniper, the list goes on and on, simply waiting to be rediscovered. Perhaps with the steady growth in artisan food culture there will also be a revival of interest and appreciation in the unharvested cornucopia of produce that the forest can offer us.

WILD MUSHROOM MOUSSE WITH A RAGOUT OF SAUTÉED MUSHROOMS

Ⓥ

WE BELIEVE IN NATURAL, HEALTHY TEXTURES AND TASTES, SO THIS MOUSSE IS NOT TOO CREAMY OR RICH. IT IS A GOOD DISH FOR ENTERTAINING AS THE MOUSSE CAN BE COOKED IN THE MORNING AND THEN GENTLY RE-HEATED FOR DINNER.

SERVES 6

FOR THE MOUSSE

120g (4½oz) fresh cèpes or 25g (1oz) dried

120g (4½oz) field mushrooms

3 tablespoons unsalted butter

1 shallot, finely chopped

1 garlic clove, finely chopped

250ml (8 fl oz) whipping cream

2 eggs

2 egg yolks

salt and freshly ground white pepper

FOR THE RAGOUT

250g (9oz) mixed fresh wild mushrooms, chanterelles, cèpes, hedgehogs, etc

2 tablespoons olive oil

2 tablespoons unsalted butter

2 tablespoons finely snipped fresh chives

TO GARNISH

6 sprigs of chervil

Pre-heat the oven to Gas Mark 1/140°C/275°F. Butter 6 ramekin dishes.

To make the mousse, scrape clean the cèpes and field mushrooms. Chop them roughly. Heat the butter in a large pan and sweat the chopped mushrooms with the shallot and garlic for about 8 minutes or until the mushrooms are nice and soft and have lost any excess moisture. Add the cream and boil for about 2 minutes until it thickens slightly. Remove from the heat and purée in a blender until you have a smooth mixture. While the blender is still turning, slowly add the eggs, the egg yolks, salt and pepper and blend for a further 10 seconds.

Fill the prepared ramekins with the mousse mixture. Cover with a small square of kitchen foil and place in a bain-marie or roasting pan half-filled with hot water. Cook for 40 minutes in the pre-heated oven or until the mousses are nicely set. Remove from the oven and set aside.

To make the ragout, pick through the wild mushrooms, trimming and scraping away any dirty or spoilt pieces. Heat the oil in a large frying-pan over high heat. When it is very hot, add the mushrooms and the butter. Fry gently for about 3–4 minutes or until the mushrooms are tender. Season with salt and pepper and turn into a colander to remove any excess liquid. To serve, tip the mousses out on to warm plates. Carefully surround with sautéed mushrooms and sprinkle on the chives. Garnish each plate with a sprig of chervil.

OVERLEAF

Left: *Blackberry Fool with Hazelnut Biscuits (page 111)*

Right: *Chargrilled Cèpes and Polenta with Rocket and Chilli-Garlic Oil (page 109)*

WILD MUSHROOM RAVIOLI WITH A MUSHROOM SOY JUS

THIS VEGETARIAN DISH IS A GOURMET'S DELIGHT. IT HAS SIMPLICITY, CLEAR FLAVOURS AND A TWIST THAT DOESN'T CLASH OR INTERFERE WITH WHAT IS MOST IMPORTANT — TASTY MUSHROOM RAVIOLI!

SERVES 4

FOR THE FILLING

65g (2½oz) shallots, chopped

120g (4½ oz) white of leek, finely chopped

1 garlic clove

1 tablespoon light olive oil

1 tablespoon butter

120g (4½oz) field or button mushrooms, sliced

120g (4½oz) wild or shiitake mushrooms

65g (2½oz) porcini mushrooms, soaked and chopped

175ml (6 fl oz) single cream

65g (2½oz) breadcrumbs

FOR THE MUSHROOM SOY JUS

175ml (6 fl oz) vegetable stock

2 tablespoons mushroom soy

½ tablespoon unsalted butter

250g (9oz) Ravioli Pasta Dough (see p. 180–1)

1 egg yolk

TO GARNISH

4 tablespoons fresh chives

4 tablespoons julienne of leek, blanched

To make the filling fry the shallots, leek and garlic with the oil and butter in a heavy-based pan over medium heat until they are soft. Add the mushrooms, cover and continue to cook until the mushrooms start to give out their moisture. Remove the lid, add the cream and simmer to reduce the juices until the mixture is quite dry. Remove from the heat and add the breadcrumbs. Chop the mixture or process in a food processor until it has a pleasant, coarse texture. Set aside.

To make the *jus*, heat the vegetable stock and the mushroom soy together in a small pan. When it comes to the boil, remove from the heat and stir in the butter. Set aside.

To make the ravioli, roll out the pasta dough as thinly as possible, or use the thinnest setting of your pasta machine. Cut out rounds with a 7.5–10cm (3–4in) circular cutter, and carefully egg wash each one with the aid of a pastry brush. Place a spoonful of the filling in the centre of each circle and fold over to form a half circle. Make sure that all the edges are sealed completely. Continue with this until you have 4–6 pieces for each person, depending on the size of your circles and whether it is to be a starter or main course portion.

Bring a large pot of salted water to the boil. Gently place in the ravioli and cook for about 3 minutes. Remove with a slotted spoon and serve immediately on warm soup plates. Pour over the warm sauce and garnish with finely snipped chives and julienne of leeks.

CHARGRILLED CÈPES AND POLENTA WITH ROCKET AND CHILLI-GARLIC OIL

THIS IS A VERY ITALIAN DISH, THE TYPE OF DISH YOU MIGHT HAVE HAD ON HOLIDAY YEARS AGO AND YOU STILL REMEMBER. WE'VE INCLUDED IT BECAUSE WITH LOCAL CÈPES AND ROCKET, WE BELIEVE THAT IT TASTES JUST AS GOOD HERE IN IRELAND.

SERVES 4

500g (1lb 2oz) fresh cèpes (or any other variety of 'boletus' mushroom)

120ml (4 fl oz) light olive oil

Salt and freshly ground white pepper

FOR THE POLENTA

1 onion, finely chopped

65g (2½oz) unsalted butter

1 litre (1¾ pints) water

250g (9oz) polenta flour

65g (2½oz) Parmesan, freshly grated

2 tablespoons olive oil

200g (7oz) rocket leaves

FOR THE CHILLI-GARLIC OIL

6 garlic cloves, peeled

4 anchovy fillets

1 tablespoon chilli flakes

½ teaspoon salt

4 tablespoons light olive oil

150ml (5 fl oz) virgin olive oil

Pre-heat the grill or chargrill to hot.

To make the polenta, fry the onion in a pan over medium heat with a little butter until soft and transparent. Add the water and bring to the boil. Gradually pour in the polenta flour, stirring all the time so that it remains smooth. Cook over medium heat for about 4–5 minutes for pre-cooked flour. (If it is not pre-cooked, follow the instructions on length of cooking time on the packet.) Stir in the Parmesan and the remaining butter. Tip the cooked polenta into a buttered tray, cover with grease-proof paper and leave to cool.

When the polenta is cool and firm, cut it into slices at least 1cm (½in) thick and brush with oil so that it is all ready for grilling.

To make the chilli-garlic oil, chop the garlic, anchovies and chilli flakes with the salt. In a small pan, heat this mixture with the light olive oil for about 5 minutes until the garlic begins to soften. Allow this infusion to cool then dilute it with the virgin olive oil (which would be damaged by the cooking process).

To prepare the cèpes, brush off any dirt with kitchen paper or a mushroom brush and scrape the stems lightly with a sharp knife. Cut the larger mushrooms into a few slices and the smaller ones simply cut in half down the middle. Brush lightly with olive oil and season with salt and pepper.

Place the cèpes on the hot grill or chargrill along with the prepared polenta slices for 3 minutes. Turn over and cook for another 3 minutes.

Dress the rocket in a little of the chilli-garlic oil. Arrange the cèpes, polenta and dressed rocket, in a casual, rustic way on each of the 4 plates and drizzle with the chilli-garlic oil.

RICE PUDDING WITH
FRUITS OF THE FOREST COMPOTE

(V)

RICE PUDDING IS ONE OF THOSE GREAT BRITISH CLASSICS. ANY MIXTURE OF BERRIES
COULD BE USED FOR A COMPOTE, AND THEIR SLIGHT TARTNESS MARRIES SO WELL WITH
THE CREAMY SUCCULENCE OF A PROPERLY MADE PUD.

SERVES 6–8

FOR THE FRESH FRUIT COMPOTE

65g (2½oz) redcurrants or
blackcurrants

120g (4½oz) blackberries

120g (4½oz) raspberries

100–150g (4–5oz) caster
sugar

dash of lemon juice

FOR THE RICE PUDDING

120g (4½oz) Arborio rice (or
pudding rice, or other short
grained rice)

1 litre (1¾ pints) milk (cream
makes a richer version, or
mix half and half)

100g (¼lb) sugar

1 tablespoon fresh lemon zest

1 vanilla pod, split

3 egg yolks

3 egg whites

50g (2oz) caster sugar

Put the berries in a small bowl, add the sugar and leave them to macerate for at least an hour. Add a dash of lemon juice and set aside.

Pre-heat the oven to Gas Mark 2/150°C/300°F.

Place the rice, milk, sugar, lemon zest, and the vanilla pod in a heavy casserole dish. Cover and place in the pre-heated oven and cook for approximately 1½–2 hours, depending on the brand and type of rice used. During this time, check the rice several times, adding more milk as necessary to keep it moist and loose. When the rice is tender to the bite, remove from the oven and allow to cool slightly.

Stir the egg yolks into the pudding. Whip the whites until firm and glossy, adding the sugar towards the end of the whipping time. Fold this into the rice mixture. Pour into a well-buttered casserole dish, and place in a bain marie. Return to the warm oven for a further 45–60

minutes, until the top is nice and golden brown.

To serve, scoop out the rice pudding onto warmed plates, and place a generous dollop of the berry compote on the side.

BLACKBERRY FOOL WITH HAZELNUT BISCUITS

Ⓥ

REMEMBER THE OLD SAYING 'THE SIMPLE THINGS ARE ALWAYS THE BEST'. WITH THE SIMPLICITY OF A FOOL AND GORGEOUS FRUIT FOR FREE, EVERYONE SHOULD BE MAKING THIS DISH! THE TASTY BISCUITS KEEP VERY WELL IN AN AIRTIGHT CONTAINER.

SERVES 4

FOR THE FOOL

300g (11oz) blackberries

75–100g (3–4oz) sugar

juice of 1 lemon

120ml (4 fl oz) double cream

50g (2oz) Mascarpone or extra 50ml (2 fl oz) double cream

FOR THE HAZELNUT BISCUITS

375g (13oz) caster sugar

250g (9oz) unsalted butter, softened

2 size 1 eggs

1 teaspoon vanilla essence

275g (10oz) plain flour

1 teaspoon bicarbonate of soda

1 teaspoon baking powder

150g (5oz) hazelnuts, roasted, peeled and chopped

To make the fool, reserve a handful of blackberries for the garnish and purée the remainder with the sugar in a blender then rub through a fine sieve. The resulting purée should be thick. The quantity of sugar relies heavily on the natural sweetness (or lack of it) of the blackberries. Add the lemon juice, then taste and adjust the flavouring.

Whisk the double cream to just soft peaks, not any thicker. Soften the Mascarpone by beating by hand and then whisk the two gently together. It is important not to overbeat this mixture. It can be taken too far and then the fool will have a grainy texture. Finally, fold this mixture together with two-thirds of the purée. The remaining one-third should be kept aside until assembly.

In a sundae dish or wine glass, place a few blackberries tossed in a spoonful of the reserved purée. Fill the glass half-way with the creamy mixture. Place a thin layer of the purée on top of this layer before filling the glass with more creamy mixture. Fill the other dishes in the same way. Chill in the fridge for at least 2 hours to firm up the mixture.

Pre-heat the oven to Gas Mark 4/180°C/350°F. Grease a baking sheet.

To make the biscuits, cream the sugar and butter together until light and fluffy. Add the eggs and vanilla essence and mix again until it is all incorporated together. Sift together the flour, bicarbonate of soda and baking powder. Fold this mixture into the butter/egg mixture. Finally, fold in the hazelnuts. Using a spoon, drop spoonfuls on to the baking sheet, leaving space between them to allow for spreading. Bake in the oven for about 8 minutes until golden brown. Remove from baking sheet and leave to cool on a wire rack.

Serve the mousse with the hazelnut biscuits and garnished with the reserved blackberries.

ELDERFLOWER AND CHAMPAGNE SORBET

EVERY TIME PAUL TASTES THIS SORBET, HE REMEMBERS THAT HE LOVES THE TASTE OF ELDERFLOWERS.
A COOL REFRESHING SORBET IS THE PERFECT CARRIER FOR ITS MUSKY FRUIT FLOWERS.
WE ALWAYS USE AN ICE-CREAM MACHINE AS IT GUARANTEES THE BEST RESULTS.

SERVES 6

300ml (10 fl oz) Sugar Syrup
(see p. 187)

grated rind and juice of
1 lemon

4 big fresh bunches of
elderflowers or 40g (1½oz)
dried

300ml (10 fl oz) Champagne

1 tablespoon egg white

Place the sugar syrup in a pan and bring to the boil. Add the lemon rind and the elderflower bunches and set aside to infuse for 20 minutes. Strain through a fine sieve and leave to cool.

Add the Champagne and lemon juice and taste for flavour. It may require a little more lemon juice. Place in an ice-cream machine with the egg white and turn according to the machine manufacturer's instructions. If you do not have a machine, spoon into a freezer tray and freeze until firm, whisking every 30 minutes to break up the ice crystals.

Serve in well chilled glasses as a refresher between courses or as a light dessert. Garnish with a sprig of mint or perhaps a few berries.

CHAPTER

11
THE HERB GARDEN

As with other foods, herbs and their uses have been passed between countries since the spread of civilization. Whether their use was primarily for medicinal or culinary purposes, fresh herbs have been part of the Irish countryside for centuries.

Many of the great estates would have cultivated a herb garden. In fact, one can see huge bushes of such herbs as rosemary, lavender, thyme and mint to name but a few, still growing in great profusion in the gardens of the National Trust houses all over the country.

Nowadays, almost every county can boast of at least half a dozen organic growers. As demand continues to increase so will supply. Fresh herbs can be quite intimidating at first, especially to those raised with only those little jars of dried ones in the house. But the only way to get one's feet wet is to plunge right in. Start with the most basic common herbs and then as confidence grows, so will the desire to understand and know more about them. There is an endless variety to choose from. Handfuls of chopped fresh parsley can finish a dish like nothing else can. Try strewing some over omelettes, salads or soups. Try using fresh sage the next time you make a stuffing or use a sprig or two of fresh thyme to flavour a meat roast or stew, or imagine throwing together your own fresh mint sauce for that Sunday roast of lamb. You will experience a different level of taste and sensation with fresh herbs. They are alive and they will lift your food off the plate.

The storing of fresh herbs is simple but important. Wrap them separately in kitchen paper and then place inside unsealed plastic bags. Keep these in the vegetable compartment of your fridge. They should last at least several days depending on the quality of their condition when you purchased them.

Of course, another alternative is to start your own little stock pile of fresh plants. Most will live quite happily in a pot on the kitchen window ledge and need very little attention other than water and sunlight. There's a multitude of books on the market about keeping herb plants; check it out for yourself.

Fresh herbs really do justify themselves and any time devoted to learning about them will be rewarded. Once you have developed a taste for them, your cooking will never be the same again.

CHERVIL AND POTATO SOUP

(V)

A LOVELY SOUP IN EARLY AUTUMN WHEN CHERVIL AND POTATOES ARE AT
THEIR BEST, THIS CAN BE VARIED WITH THE ADDITION OF CHICKEN, SMOKED SALMON, MUSHROOMS
OR OTHER FAVOURITE INGREDIENTS.

SERVES 8

50g (2oz) unsalted butter

300g (11oz) onions, chopped

salt and freshly ground white pepper

1 large bunch fresh chervil, about 150g (5oz)

300g (11oz) floury potatoes, peeled and diced

1 bouquet garni

2 litres (3½ pints) chicken stock or water

100ml (3½ fl oz) whipping cream, lightly whipped

sprigs of chervil to garnish

Melt the butter in a large pan over low heat and fry the onions with a little salt for 10 minutes. Meanwhile, finely chop the chervil stalks, reserving the leaves. Add the potatoes, the chervil stalks, bouquet garni and the chicken stock to the pan and bring to the boil. Simmer for 20 minutes.

Remove from the heat and allow to cool for 15 minutes. Discard the bouquet garni. Add the chervil leaves. Purée in a blender and pass through a fine mesh sieve. Check the seasoning, adding salt and white pepper as necessary.

Heat the soup gently without allowing it to boil. Ladle into warm bowls and garnish with a dollop of cream and a sprig of chervil.

ARTICHOKE RAVIOLI WITH BASIL PESTO

BASIL PESTO IS ONE OF THOSE FOODS JUST BURSTING WITH FLAVOUR. ITS SENSUAL AROMA LIFTS ANYTHING IT'S SERVED WITH TO DIZZYING HEIGHTS OF TASTE SENSATION!

SERVES 4

FOR THE PASTA DOUGH

500g (1lb 2oz) plain flour

4 eggs

5 egg yolks

salt

3 tablespoons vegetable oil

2 tablespoons water

FOR THE FILLING

2 large artichokes

1 tablespoon unsalted butter

1 tablespoon chopped onion

1 garlic clove

50g (2oz) button mushrooms, sliced

2 tablespoons breadcrumbs

salt and freshly ground black pepper

1 egg, lightly beaten

1 tablespoon olive oil

FOR THE BASIL PESTO

40g (1½oz) pine nuts

3 garlic cloves

120ml (4 fl oz) virgin olive oil

120–150g (4½–5oz) fresh basil leaves

25g (1oz) Parmesan

salt and freshly ground black pepper

To make the pasta dough, mix together all the ingredients in a bowl or in a mixer or processor until they have all come together in a smooth coherent mass. As flours vary, more water or more flour may need to be added until the consistency is right.

Roll out the dough by hand or on a pasta machine until very thin. The dough will be a little softer and more pliable than a normal pasta dough. This is needed so that it can be shaped around the filling. Lay each sheet of pasta on to a tray, layering between cling film. A damp towel over the top will help prevent the sheets from drying out. Set aside.

To make the filling, carefully trim all the outside leaves from the artichokes with a very sharp knife until you are left with only the artichoke heart. Simmer the artichokes in boiling water for about 20 minutes or until tender. Leave to cool in the cooking liquid. Remove the hairy choke from the centre of the artichokes and set one aside for later. Chop the other one roughly and set aside for the moment.

In a pan, melt the butter and fry the onion and garlic until soft and lightly brown. Add the sliced mushrooms and cook until most of the moisture has evaporated and the mushrooms are well cooked. Tip the mushroom mixture into a food processor and pulse until you have a coarse mixture, or chop finely. Add the artichokes, breadcrumbs, salt and pepper and pulse again or mix together just to re-incorporate all the ingredients together. Scrape the mixture into a bowl and when it is cool, add the egg.

To make the basil pesto, put the pine nuts, garlic and olive oil into a blender and process until fairly smooth. Add the basil leaves, Parmesan, salt and pepper and process again until the leaves are completely incorporated.

To assemble the ravioli, cut the pasta in 5cm (2in) squares and lay them out on a work surface. Brush the top of half of the squares with egg wash then spoon a dollop of the filling on to the centre of each square. Carefully cover these with the remaining squares, pressing gently to seal all the edges of each one.

Slice the remaining artichoke into small pieces and sauté in olive oil until lightly browned.

Cook the ravioli in plenty of boiling, salted water for 2 minutes then lift them out and drain well. Serve the ravioli on warm plates, scatter on the slices of sautéed artichoke and drizzle the basil pesto generously over it.

SORREL SOUFFLÉ WITH FRESH TOMATO SAUCE

SORREL HAS A GREAT AFFINITY FOR EGGS, ITS SHARPNESS BALANCING AND COUNTERACTING THE RICHNESS OF THE YOLKS. THIS IS A GREAT TOMATO SAUCE TO KNOW AS IT IS SIMPLE AND QUICK.

SERVES 4

50g (2oz) unsalted butter

500g (1lb 2oz) sorrel, trimmed and chopped

3 eggs, separated

100g (4oz) white bread, crusts removed, soaked in milk, squeezed and chopped

4 tablespoons freshly grated Parmesan

salt and freshly ground white pepper

FOR THE TOMATO SAUCE

2 tablespoons finely chopped shallots

120g (4½oz) unsalted butter, diced

1 tablespoon tomato purée

6 plum tomatoes, skinned, seeded and chopped

Pre-heat the oven to Gas Mark 5/190°C/375°F. Butter 4 × 200ml (7 fl oz) soufflé ramekins.

To make the tomato sauce, fry the shallots gently in 1 tablespoon of butter in a stainless steel pan for 3 minutes over moderate heat, without letting them take any colour. Add the tomato purée and chopped tomatoes and cook for about 5 minutes or until the tomato pieces have wilted and the sauce is just starting to thicken. Whisk in the diced butter, 1 tablespoon at a time. Season with salt and pepper and set aside.

To make the soufflé, melt the butter in a stainless steel pan and cook the sorrel over low heat for about 3 minutes until it is completely soft. Beat the egg yolks and mix in with the sorrel. Add the soaked bread and mix thoroughly.

Coat the prepared ramekins lightly with the Parmesan. Beat the egg whites together with a pinch of salt until they are very stiff but not grainy. Fold into the sorrel mixture and turn in to the ramekins.

Bake in the pre-heated oven for about 15 minutes until well risen and nicely browned on top. Serve immediately with the fresh tomato sauce on the side.

ROAST SEA BASS WITH A PARSLEY AND CAPER SAUCE

SEA BASS IS A PROTECTED SPECIES IN SOUTHERN IRELAND AND IT IS RARELY SEEN IN NORTHERN WATERS. IF YOU ARE LUCKY ENOUGH TO CATCH ONE YOURSELF, TREAT THIS SPECIAL FISH WITH RESPECT AND COOK IT SIMPLY.

SERVES 4

600g (1lb 5oz) sea bass fillets, scaled and boneless

salt and freshly ground white pepper

100g (4oz) plain flour

120ml (4½fl oz) virgin olive oil

3 tablespoons chopped fresh parsley

2 tablespoons capers

4 anchovy fillets

1 garlic clove, chopped

1 teaspoon Dijon mustard

1 tablespoon lemon juice

Trim the sea bass, check it for bones and scales and portion it evenly into 4 portions. Season the fillets generously with salt and pepper and lightly dust in the flour.

Heat 2 tablespoons of olive oil in a large frying-pan (preferably non-stick) and sauté the sea bass over a medium heat for about 5 minutes on each side.

While the sea bass is cooking, grind the parsley, capers, anchovies and garlic with a mortar and pestle or in a food processor. Finally, when it is fairly well mixed together, add the mustard, lemon juice and remaining virgin olive oil. Season with pepper and check it for salt.

To serve, spoon some of the sauce on to each of the warm plates and carefully set the sea bass on top. Serve with steamed new potatoes and a green salad.

RACK OF PORK WITH GRILLED VEGETABLES AND HERBES DE PROVENCE

USE A SELECTION OF VEGETABLES IN SEASON FOR THIS DISH, MAKING SURE THEY ARE GOOD QUALITY.

SERVES 4

1 rack of pork, about 900g (2lb) with 4–5 rib bones

2 tablespoons sea salt

1 tablespoon freshly ground black pepper

250ml (8 fl oz) light olive oil

HERBES DE PROVENCE

2 tablespoons chopped fresh parsley

1 tablespoon chopped fresh thyme

1 tablespoon chopped fresh rosemary

1 teaspoon chopped fresh sage

1 teaspoon dried oregano

2 bay leaves, crushed

FOR THE DRESSING

250ml (8 fl oz) virgin olive oil

juice of 1 lemon

1 teaspoon salt

1 teaspoon black peppercorns, cracked

FOR THE VEGETABLES

about 900g (2lb) mixed vegetables such as aubergine, courgettes, red onions, mushrooms, leeks, carrots or potatoes (use what is in season and available in a good quality)

120ml (4 fl oz) olive oil

Trim the rack of pork of skin and clean the meat from between the bones to expose the bones, nice and clean. Mix together all the herbes de provence ingredients. Rub the salt, black pepper and 2 tablespoons of the mixed herbs into the pork rack and then cover and put in the fridge for at least 4–8 hours.

Approximately 50 minutes before dinner time, light the barbecue chargrill or pre-heat the grill. Take the pork out of the fridge, drain off any juices and lightly pat dry. When the barbecue or grill is hot, drizzle a little olive oil over the pork and put it on a moderate part of the barbecue. Cook for about 30 minutes, turning and basting it with a little oil from time to time.

Leave to rest for about 5–10 minutes off the heat to allow the juices to settle.

Place all the ingredients for the dressing in a small bowl and mix thoroughly. Add 2 tablespoons of the herb mixture and allow to stand while you prepare the vegetables.

Cut the vegetables into attractive shapes and sizes but make sure that they are not so small that they will fall through the racks of the barbecue. Toss the vegetables in olive oil and sprinkle with the remaining herbs and a little salt and pepper.

When it's about 10 minutes time from eating, start to cook the vegetables on the hottest part of the grill. Watch them very carefully, turning them once or twice before removing them to a warm plate.

To serve, carve the rack of pork into 4 large cutlets. Arrange enough vegetables for each person on each plate, place the cutlet in the centre, drizzle the whole plate with the herb dressing and serve.

WARM PARSLEY SALAD WITH HARICOT BEANS AND TONGUE

THIS DISH IS BEST MADE WITH YOUNG FRESH PARSLEY. BOTH THE CURLY
AND FLAT LEAF VARIETIES WORK EQUALLY WELL.

SERVES 4

150g (5oz) haricot beans, rinsed

2 tablespoons onion, chopped

2 tablespoons carrot, chopped

$\frac{1}{2}$ bay leaf

salt

1 large bunch parsley leaves, washed

6 tablespoons Vinaigrette Dressing (see page 177)

freshly ground black pepper

250g (9oz) cooked ox tongue, sliced into 2cm ($\frac{3}{4}$in) batons

Place the beans in a bowl and pour enough water over them to cover generously. Let them soak overnight. Rinse the beans, and place them in a medium saucepan, covered by 2cm ($\frac{3}{4}$in) of cold water. Bring to the boil and simmer for 1 hour.

Add the onion, carrot, and bay leaf and salt and simmer for 1 hour, or until the beans are beginning to burst. Allow the beans to cool for about 5 minutes, then add the parsley leaves, vinaigrette, and the pepper.

To serve, spoon the bean and parsley mixture onto warm plates, and sprinkle the chopped tongue on top.

OVERLEAF

Left: *Fruit Gâteau with Lemon Balm (page 124)*

Right: *Rack of Pork with Grilled Vegetables and Herbes de Provence (page 120)*

FRUIT GÂTEAU WITH LEMON BALM

THIS MAKES FOR A DELIGHTFULLY LIGHT DESSERT, AS REFRESHING AS A SORBET ON
THE PALATE YET THAT MUCH MORE IN TEXTURE AND APPEARANCE. IT COULD JUST AS EASILY
BE MADE IN A TERRINE AND THEN SLICED INTO PORTIONS.

SERVES 6

1 bottle of dry Muscat wine

300ml (10 fl oz) Sugar Syrup
(see p. 187)

1 bunch fresh lemon balm

4 large grapefruit

8 navel oranges

8 leaves gelatine or agar-agar,
soaked in cold water for 10
minutes

FOR THE SAUCE

300ml (10 fl oz) fresh orange
juice, strained

100g (4oz) caster sugar

$\frac{1}{2}$ tablespoon arrowroot or
potato flour

3 tablespoons water

2 tablespoons grenadine

lemon balm or mint to garnish

Gently infuse the wine, sugar syrup and half of the lemon balm leaves in a large pan over a medium heat for about 20 minutes.

Meanwhile, cut away the skin and pith from the grapefruits and oranges. Neatly slice out the segments so that no membrane is left on. Catch the juices and segments in a bowl as you are doing this. It is very important to lay the segments out on a towel or kitchen paper now to let the individual segments dry. If you don't do this, the jelly will have trouble adhering to the segments and the whole thing may fall apart when you demould it.

Add the softened gelatine or agar-agar to the infusion and stir until it is well dissolved. Strain through a very fine sieve. Allow to cool to room temperature, but it must still be pourable.

Grease 6 little cups or moulds with a grease spray. Pour just enough of the infusion into each one to cover the base to a depth of about 2–3mm ($\frac{1}{8}$in). Carefully lay 2 or 3 leaves of lemon balm on to this layer. Bear in mind that when presented, the bottom of the mould will be on top, so place the leaves in upside down, with the vein side facing up.

Taking the orange and grapefruit segments, lay them on to this base, alternating the two to provide a juxtaposition of the colours. Place them in rather tightly, not pressing them down or in, just making them fit snugly together. Ladle or pour in the infusion, letting it fill all the gaps. Gently tap the mould once or twice to remove any air bubbles and fill up each mould to the rim. Place in the fridge for at least 2 hours until the moulds are set completely.

To make the sauce, put the orange juice and sugar in a small pan and bring to the boil over a medium high heat. Mix the arrowroot or potato flour to a smooth paste with the water then stir it into the pan and return to the boil. Let simmer for 1 minute just to ensure that the arrowroot or potato flour is well dissolved. Remove from heat and strain through a fine sieve. Add the grenadine and chill in the fridge. The chilled sauce should not be too thick in consistency, yet not too runny either.

Un-mould the little gâteau on to each plate by running a very sharp knife around the edge of the mould and, if necessary, quickly dipping the mould into very hot water. This slightly melts the jelly, releasing the edges and bottom from the mould. Surround with the chilled grenadine sauce and garnish with a sprig of lemon balm or mint.

RED WINE AND FRESH THYME POACHED FIGS

To prepare fruits with a 'savoury' herb is not at all a new idea: pear and basil is a well known example. Jeanne feels that fresh thyme draws out the 'tobaccoey' essence of the figs, enhancing the deep and earthy flavour.

SERVES 4

$\frac{1}{2}$ bottle (750ml/1$\frac{1}{4}$ pints) ruby port

$\frac{1}{2}$ bottle (750ml/1$\frac{1}{4}$ pints) red wine

350ml (23$\frac{1}{2}$ fl oz) Sugar Syrup (see page 187)

$\frac{1}{2}$ lemon

4 sprigs fresh thyme

$\frac{1}{2}$ vanilla pod

12 fresh ripe figs

TO GARNISH

almonds, flaked or toasted

Place the port and red wine in a large saucepan and bring to the boil. Continue to boil until the liquid has reduced by half. Add the syrup, lemon, fresh thyme, and vanilla pod and return to the boil. Gently place the figs in a single layer in the saucepan, and cover with greaseproof paper. Simmer over a gentle heat for 5 minutes, and remove from the heat.

Remove the figs, thyme and lemon, and cover them. Meanwhile, reduce the liquid by half. Pour the concentrated poaching liquid back over the figs, and let them steep together overnight in the fridge. If desired, the liquid can again be reduced to a thick syrupy consistency that would coat the back of a spoon. Don't put the thyme or lemon in during this reduction, as their flavours could become too strong.

To serve, place 3 figs on each serving plate, and serve with crème fraîche, or a vanilla or almond ice-cream also goes well. Garnish with a few flaked or toasted almonds if desired.

CHAPTER

12

THE VEGETABLE GARDEN

VEGETABLES IN THEIR own right must be, by tradition, one of the most neglected foods in
Ireland. They constitute by far the most varied
and abundant source of nourishment, yet have been rel-
egated to mere accompaniment status for far too long.
Happily, things are now changing, slowly but surely. The
widespread habit of holidaying on the Continent as well
as the Europeans coming to Ireland for their holidays,
have helped open the eyes of the general public over the
last twenty years or so.

Historically, it was only the great estates with their
walled gardens that delved into the growing of various
vegetables, experimenting with varieties and so on. The
average farm may have grown a few spuds, perhaps some
swedes, some cabbage, maybe even some leeks, but on
the whole they were very basic. Part of the problem lies
in the climate. A late start and an early finish to the
growing season is not that conducive, neither is the
dampness, and in many parts of the country, the soil is
just too heavy to offer good growing conditions. Paul
really finds, though, that those vegetables grown locally
in season do have a superb flavour, due to the slow and
natural growing. In fact, he claims that they are as good

in quality as any of those we have bought in London, Australia or even California. With the developing interest there is these days, hopefully the demand will encourage more growers to overcome these regional difficulties.

In general, there is a definite lack of knowledge of vegetables and ways to prepare and cook them. People usually tend to overcook them, draining away flavour, texture and goodness. Personally, we find great inspi-

ration in vegetables, their variety and their natural seasons. Taking each harvest's bounty, the options are endless. One can boil or steam, pan-fry or deep-fry, bake or braise, batter or stuff. Obviously different vegetables suit different techniques better than others, but just remember to treat each one with the care and respect it deserves. A wide variety ensures a healthy body, whether there is also meat in the diet or not. Let the humble vegetable take centre stage on your dinner plate. The more you cook with them, the more you will grow to appreciate their versatility and flavours.

TRIO OF STUFFED VEGETABLES

STUFFED VEGETABLES ARE VERY VERSATILE, THEY MAKE GREAT STARTERS OR MAIN COURSE ACCOMPANIMENTS. HERE I'VE PUT THREE TOGETHER FOR A SUPERB VEGETARIAN MAIN COURSE.

ARTICHOKE STUFFED WITH CREAMED AUBERGINE

SERVES 2

2 tablespoons olive oil

2 tablespoons white wine vinegar

1 litre (1¾ pints) water

1 tablespoon salt

2 medium artichokes

FOR THE FILLING

1 medium aubergine

salt and freshly ground white pepper

125ml (4½ fl oz) olive oil

1 tablespoon unsalted butter

150g (5oz) shiitake mushrooms, trimmed

1 garlic clove, finely chopped

250ml (8 fl oz) whipping cream

1 tablespoon chopped fresh parsley (optional)

Mix the oil, vinegar, water and salt in a pan. This is the cooking liquid. Carefully trim all the outside leaves from the artichokes with a very sharp knife until you are left with only the artichoke heart. Simmer the artichokes in the cooking liquid for about 20 minutes or until they are tender. Allow them to cool in the cooking liquid.

To make the filling, trim and chop the aubergine into 1cm (½in) square pieces. Season with salt and pepper. Fry gently in the olive oil until golden brown and quite soft to the touch. Drain in a sieve.

Melt the butter and fry the mushrooms and garlic with a little salt and pepper. When the mushrooms are soft, add the cream and the aubergines and simmer for about 3–5 minutes until the cream thickens.

When the artichokes are cool, remove the hairy chokes from the centre with a small spoon. Heap the filling into each artichoke heart. Top with chopped parsley, if you like, for some colour.

TOMATO STUFFED WITH SPINACH

2 ripe thick-fleshed tomatoes

120g (4½oz) fresh spinach

1 garlic clove

2 tablespoons unsalted butter

a pinch of freshly grated nutmeg

salt and freshly ground black pepper

finely crushed croûtons or breadcrumbs to garnish

Trim a 5mm (¼in) slice off the top of each tomato and carefully scoop out the inside with a teaspoon. Pick over and wash the spinach, removing any tough stalks. Peel the garlic clove and skewer on the tips of a kitchen fork. Heat the butter in a frying-pan until it is golden brown. Add the spinach all at once. Stir immediately, with the 'garlic fork', add the nutmeg, salt and pepper and continue cooking for about 2–4 minutes until the spinach is bright green and quite tender but not shapeless. Drain off and discard any excess moisture from the spinach then pile it into the tomatoes. Top with the crushed croûtons or breadcrumbs.

COURGETTE STUFFED WITH RATATOUILLE

1 beautiful courgette, about 13–15cm (5–6in)

1 small onion, finely chopped

1 garlic clove, crushed

250ml (8 fl oz) olive oil

120g (4½oz) aubergine, finely diced

120g (4½oz) courgette, finely diced

1 small red pepper, finely diced

salt and freshly ground black pepper

fresh herbs to garnish

Cut the courgette lengthwise and scoop out the centre to make a hollow boat shape. Blanch in boiling water for 1 minute. Refresh with cold water and drain.

Fry the onion and garlic in a little of the olive oil, until soft. Fry the aubergine, courgette and red pepper, each separately, in olive oil and drain each of excess olive oil as they are cooked. Carefully mix all the ingredients together and season with salt and pepper. Pile into the courgette 'boats'.

Pre-heat the oven to Gas Mark 4/180°C/350°F.

Put all the stuffed vegetables on a baking tray and warm them in the pre-heated oven for about 10 minutes. Present a trio of each on separate plates. Garnish with fresh herbs.

OVERLEAF

Left: *Trio of Stuffed Vegetables* (pages 128–9)

Centre: *Asparagus and Wild Mushroom Bruschetta* (page 133)

Right: *Champ* (page 139)

WARM SALAD OF GRILLED VEGETABLES WITH PARMESAN AND BALSAMIC VINEGAR

THIS IS A SUMMER DISH WHICH WAS INSPIRED ORIGINALLY BY THE EXCELLENT PRODUCE WE USED TO WORK WITH IN CALIFORNIA. THE FUNNY THING IS THAT IT TASTES JUST AS GOOD IN IRELAND WITH OUR OWN WONDERFUL, LOCAL SUMMER VEGETABLES.

SERVES 6

1 red pepper

1 yellow pepper

100ml (3½fl oz) light olive oil

1 courgette

1 aubergine

6 large mushrooms

1 red onion

1 artichoke heart, choke removed

3 small leeks, split and washed

salt and freshly ground black pepper

a selection of salad leaves

100ml (3½fl oz) virgin olive oil

50ml (2fl oz) balsamic vinegar

100g (4oz) Parmesan, shaved with a peeler

1 tablespoon chopped fresh thyme

1 tablespoon chopped fresh parsley

1 tablespoon black peppercorns, cracked

To prepare the vegetables, rub the peppers with a little light olive oil and roast them under a very hot grill (or in a very hot oven) until the skins are blackening. Peel, seed and slice each one into 6 pieces. Slice the courgette and aubergine into 1cm (½in) slices and drizzle lightly with light olive oil.

Cut the onion and the artichoke heart into 6 wedges. Blanch the onion wedges and the leeks in a pan of boiling salted water for 2 minutes each and refresh them under cold water.

Pre-heat the grill. Arrange all the vegetables separately on grill trays and brush lightly with olive oil. Season with salt and pepper. Grill each vegetable separately until just cooked. The peppers and the artichoke only really need 1–2 minutes while the mushrooms, onion, courgette and aubergines will take about 5 minutes each.

To serve, arrange the vegetables attractively on the plates and place a few mixed salad leaves in the centre of each arrangement. Drizzle with the virgin olive oil and the balsamic vinegar. Sprinkle with the Parmesan, herbs and black pepper.

ASPARAGUS AND WILD MUSHROOM BRUSCHETTA

THIS MAY NOT BE A LOCAL DISH BUT YOU CAN GROW GREAT ASPARAGUS IN IRELAND AND WE HAVE PLENTY OF WILD MUSHROOMS. BRUSCHETTA IS A PEASANT-STYLE ITALIAN DISH WHICH THE IRISH REALLY ENJOY. THERE ARE PLENTY OF WAYS YOU CAN VARY THE DISH TO SUIT YOUR OWN TASTE. YOU CAN USE FRESH PARMESAN AS A GARNISH, FOR EXAMPLE, GRILL THE BREAD AND ASPARAGUS FOR EXTRA FLAVOUR, OR SUBSTITUTE CHICKEN, PORK OR FENNEL FOR THE ASPARAGUS. ANY LEFT-OVER DUXELLE CAN BE FROZEN.

SERVES 4

FOR THE DUXELLE

120g (4½oz) onion, chopped

3 garlic cloves, crushed

120ml (4 fl oz) olive oil

450g (1lb) button mushrooms, roughly chopped

65g (2½oz) dried porcini, soaked for 30 minutes then drained

salt and freshly ground black pepper

4 tablespoons truffle or olive oil

FOR THE BRUSCHETTA

4 slices country bread or baguette

olive oil

1 garlic clove (optional)

FOR THE ASPARAGUS

450g (1lb) asparagus spears

TO GARNISH

a few sautéed mushrooms or wild mushrooms

a few salad leaves

sprigs of fresh parsley or chervil (optional)

To make the duxelle, fry the onion and garlic in the oil in a large pan until soft and transparent. Add the mushrooms and porcini and cook for about 10 minutes. Allow the mixture to cool a little before chopping or processing in a food processor until coarsely chopped. It should not be too fine; there should be texture and shape left in the mushrooms. Season generously with salt and pepper and a little of the truffle or olive oil.

To make the bruschetta, pre-heat the grill. Brush each side of the bread or baguette with a little olive oil. If you like garlic, you may want to rub each slice with a peeled clove as well. Toast under the pre-heated grill (or in a hot oven) until crisp.

To cook the asparagus, break off any very tough parts of the asparagus and if the skin is tough, peel the stalks carefully. Cook in boiling salted water for 4–8 minutes, depending on size. Drain carefully and set aside.

To serve, spread the hot mushroom duxelle generously on the sliced, toasted bread and set in the middle of warm plates. Top with the asparagus spears and drizzle the whole thing with the remaining truffle or olive oil. Garnish with sautéed mushrooms, a few salad leaves, or sprigs of parsley or chervil, if liked.

Cos Salad

This is Paul's version of caesar salad. Done properly, with first-class ingredients, it is everyone's favourite salad. Always use good quality anchovies and olives for the best flavour. You can use a food processor for the dressing. It is worth making your own garlic croûtons as they are so much better than store-bought.

SERVES 4–6

FOR THE DRESSING

$\frac{1}{2}$ teaspoon salt

1 tablespoon Dijon mustard

50ml (2 fl oz) lemon juice

1 garlic clove, crushed

2 tablespoons Worcestershire sauce

10 drops tabasco sauce

4 anchovies

200ml (7 fl oz) light olive oil

FOR THE CROÛTONS

6 slices dense bread

6 tablespoons olive oil

2 garlic cloves

1 large cos lettuce, washed

100g (4oz) Parmesan, grated

black olives

To make the dressing, dissolve the salt and mustard in the lemon juice. Add the crushed garlic, Worcestershire sauce and tabasco sauce. Crush the anchovy fillets through a garlic press, then add them to the bowl. Slowly whisk in the olive oil, a drop at a time, so that it gradually incorporates into the rest of the mixture. Taste and adjust the seasoning as preferred.

Pre-heat the oven to Gas Mark 3/160°C/325°F.

To make garlic croûtons, drizzle or brush the bread slices on both sides with olive oil and toast in the pre-heated oven for about 10 minutes until crisp and golden. When you remove them from the oven, while they are still hot, rub a peeled clove of garlic all over both sides, then cut into cubes.

To serve, tear the bigger outer leaves of the lettuce roughly and use the small inside ones whole. Toss them with the dressing and two-thirds of the grated Parmesan.

Attractively arrange a big pile in the centre of each plate and garnish with as many of the garlic croûtons and black olives as you fancy. Top it all off with the remaining Parmesan.

SPICED PUMPKIN PIE WITH CINNAMON CREAM

PUMPKIN HAS A FINE DELICATE FLAVOUR THAT TOO MANY PEOPLE MISS OUT ON BY CARELESS COOKING. BY BAKING THE FLESH IN ITS OWN SHELL, THE NATURAL SWEETNESS IS INTENSIFIED, THE TEXTURE IS UNADULTERATED AND THE FLAVOUR CAN REALLY SPEAK OUT.

SERVES 8

200g (7oz) Sweet Shortcrust Pastry (see p. 184)

1 egg yolk, for eggwashing pastry

1 medium pumpkin

200g (7oz) soft brown sugar

4 size 1 eggs, lightly beaten

$1\frac{1}{2}$ teaspoons ground cinnamon

$\frac{1}{2}$ teaspoon freshly grated nutmeg

1 teaspoon ground ginger

$\frac{1}{4}$ teaspoon ground cloves

$\frac{1}{4}$ teaspoon salt

1 tablespoon freshly grated ginger root

175ml (6 fl oz) double cream

3 tablespoons brandy or cognac

FOR THE CINNAMON CREAM

250ml (8 fl oz) whipping cream

100g (4oz) caster sugar

1 tablespoon ground cinnamon

Pre-heat the oven to Gas Mark 4/180°C/350°F. Lightly grease a 20cm (8in) pie dish with sloping sides.

To prepare the tart base roll out the pastry to a thickness of about 3mm ($\frac{1}{8}$in) and use to line the prepared pie dish. Chill in the fridge for 20 minutes. Cover with grease-proof paper, fill with baking beans and bake blind in the pre-heated oven for 12 minutes or until the base is a light golden brown. Remove from oven, remove the paper and beans and brush the inside with the egg wash to seal the pastry. Set aside.

To prepare the pumpkin, cut it in half, scoop out and discard the seeds and stringy bits and place the pumpkin in a roasting pan, shell side up. Bake this in the pre-heated oven for about 1 hour or until it is tender and falling apart. Scrape the cooked flesh off the shell and press through a sieve. The sieved flesh should be quite dry. Measure out 350ml (12 fl oz).

Whisk together the sugar, eggs and spices until well dissolved. Stir in the pumpkin flesh, then the cream and stir until smooth. Finally, add the brandy or cognac and taste. Pour the mixture into the pre-baked pie shell and cook in the pre-heated oven for about 30–35 minutes until set. Remove from the oven and leave to cool. It will continue to firm and set as it cools.

To prepare the cinnamon cream, whisk the cream until it holds soft peaks. Add the sugar and cinnamon and whisk again until they have dissolved. The cream should just hold firm peaks. It should be mildly sweet and fragrant with the taste and aroma of cinnamon. Chill until it is required.

To serve the pie, cut it into wedges and serve garnished with a generous dollop of the cinnamon cream. This pie tastes best when just slightly warm or at room temperature rather than chilled.

CARROT CAKE

In North America, almost every household would have their own version of carrot cake with slightly varying ingredients, from pineapple to raisins. Why not? The important thing here is that the carrot gives the cake moisture, sweetness and a terrific keeping quality. Fresh, tasty carrots give the best results.

SERVES 10–12

250g (9oz) unsalted butter

375g (13oz) caster sugar

grated rind of 2 oranges

4 eggs

450g (1lb) carrots, grated

150g (5oz) almonds or pecans, chopped

1 tablespoon vanilla essence

juice of 1 orange

250g (9oz) plain flour

2 teaspoons bicarbonate of soda

1 teaspoon mixed spice

1 teaspoon salt

FOR THE ICING

225g (8oz) full-fat soft cheese, at room temperature

65g (2½oz) unsalted butter, at room temperature

400g (14oz) icing sugar, sifted

1 teaspoon vanilla essence

Pre-heat the oven to Gas Mark 4/180°C/350°F. Grease a 23cm (9in) spring-form cake tin.

Beat the butter, sugar and orange rind until they are light and fluffy. Slowly add the eggs, beating well to incorporate each addition fully before adding more. Fold in the grated carrot and chopped nuts. Add the vanilla essence and orange juice. Finally, sift the flour, bicarbonate of soda, spice and salt together then fold into the cake mixture.

Pour the mixture into the prepared spring-form tin and bake in the pre-heated oven for about 45–60 minutes. The sides of the cake should be coming away from the sides of the cake tin and a skewer inserted into the centre of the cake should come out clean.

To make the icing, cream the cheese and the butter together until smooth. Add the icing sugar and vanilla essence and beat until smooth. This frosting is rich, thick and delicious. Spread the icing generously over the top of the cake.

CHAPTER

13
THE POTATO FIELD

THE POTATO WAS introduced to Ireland in the 1700s. Less than one hundred years later, nearly all labourers and their families were dependent on it for subsistence. The disaster brought on by blight destroying the entire crop in 1845, is only too well known. The Great Famine is now only a part of Ireland's history and the potato is a source of pride and importance to most Irishmen. Pride, because Ireland is one of the last few places still bothering to grow varieties long lost on the British mainland to those two 'virtues', yield and profit. Importance, because the Irish truly love their potatoes; most would admit to eating them at least once a day.

A potato is not just a potato. This was something that Jeanne, grown up on the Canadian prairies, never really understood until she moved to Ireland. What makes a good baking potato compared to a good salad potato? Which is best for frying and which is good for mashing? Several years later she's not only appreciating the difference, she's demanding it! The floury Maris Piper makes the best chips around. The Kerr's Pink are great for mashed potato. Salads require a firmer, more waxy potato like the Pentland Squire or the foreign varieties

like the Bintje or the Ratte. Selecting potatoes isn't easy but it is worth the effort. Two of the best known Irish potato dishes are Champ (also known as Stelk) made with spring onions and Colcannon, made with cabbage.

Another traditional method of cooking is simply boiling them in their jackets. This not only holds the potatoes in shape but it keeps in the goodness as well. The potato must also be one of the most popular soup vegetables, adding texture, substance and flavour.

Storing potatoes properly also needs a bit of care and thought. Be sure to remove them from those plastic bags in which the supermarket sells them. Keep them in a cool, dry and dark place. Best of all, get out to the country to buy direct from a farmer if you can.

CHAMP

WE LIKE TO EAT CHAMP AS A DISH ON ITS OWN, WHICH IS REALLY THE PROPER WAY. FOR US, IT IS
THE ULTIMATE COMFORT FOOD, REMINDING US OF CHILDHOOD, SCHOOL LUNCHES AND MUM.

SERVES 4

1kg (2¼lb) floury potatoes
(Kerr's Pink, King Edwards,
Désirée, etc)

6 large spring onions

300ml (10 fl oz) full cream
milk

4 tablespoons unsalted butter

salt

Peel and quarter the potatoes. Place them in a large pan, cover with salted water and bring to the boil. Simmer for 20–30 minutes until the potatoes are just cooked. Pour off the water, cover the pan and let it sit for about 3 minutes; this allows the potatoes to become soft and completely cooked.

While the potatoes are resting, wash and finely chop the spring onions. Combine the milk and butter in a small pan and bring to the boil. Put the chopped onions into the boiling mixture, then remove from the heat and let them infuse for 1 minute. This mellows out the raw onion taste. Mash the potatoes, then stir in the milk mixture until the whole mixture is smooth. Check seasoning and add salt if necessary. Serve on its own in warm bowls with a spoonful of butter on top.

COLCANNON

COLCANNON IS TO THE SOUTH OF IRELAND WHAT CHAMP IS TO THE NORTH,
A COMFORT FOOD, A WARM, SATISFYING, HOMELY DISH. THIS IS EUGENE O'CALLAGHAN'S –
OF EUGENE'S RESTAURANT IN COUNTY WEXFORD – OLD FAMILY RECIPE.

SERVES 6

600g (1½lb) floury potatoes,
peeled and quartered

2–3 medium onions
(300g/11oz), finely chopped

½ white cabbage, cored, finely
sliced

2 large parsnips

1 teaspoon salt

3 large cabbage leaves

Line the bottom of a deep heavy-bottomed saucepan with quartered potatoes. On top of this, place a layer of onions, then a layer of cabbage, then a layer of parsnips. Repeat this again until all the ingredients are used up. Place the salt in 300ml (½ pint) of water and pour in. Top it all off with the cabbage leaves. Cover with a lid and gently bring to the boil. Cook gently for approximately 1 hour. Remove the cabbage leaves from the top, and roughly mash all the cooked vegetables together. Serve with lots of butter and freshly chopped parsley.

POTATO TORTE WITH CABBAGE, BACON AND CHEDDAR

THIS TASTY TORTE CAN BE A LUNCHEON DISH IN ITS OWN RIGHT SERVED WITH
A GREEN SALAD, OR IT CAN BE USED AS AN ACCOMPANIMENT.

SERVES 8

$\frac{1}{2}$ Savoy cabbage, outer leaves removed, cored and finely sliced

200g (7oz) streaky bacon, cut into 1cm ($\frac{1}{2}$in) pieces

30g (1$\frac{1}{4}$oz) butter

700g (1$\frac{1}{2}$lb) potatoes

salt and freshly ground black pepper

200g (7oz) Cheddar cheese, grated

Pre-heat the oven to Gas Mark 6/200°C/400°F.

Cook the Savoy cabbage in 1 litre (1$\frac{3}{4}$ pints) of boiling water for 2 minutes. Refresh in cold water, and dry thoroughly.

Sauté the bacon in the butter in a heavy skillet over a medium heat until the bacon is just starting to brown. Remove the bacon from the fat. Reserve the fat, and toss the bacon with the cabbage.

Peel and slice the potatoes to a 4mm ($\frac{1}{8}$in) thickness. Rinse and dry the potato slices and season them lightly with salt and pepper. Then toss them in the bacon fat.

In a non-stick pan or baking dish arrange a layer of potatoes on the bottom, and sprinkle lightly with some of the cheese. Top this with a layer of cabbage and bacon, and again sprinkle lightly with cheese. Continue building the torte in this fashion until all the ingredients are

used up. It is important that each layer is sprinkled with cheese, as this helps to hold the torte together.

Cover the pan with a circle of greaseproof paper, and bake in the oven for 45 minutes. Remove from the oven and allow to cool to room temperature. Remove the greaseproof paper, and turn the torte out onto a cutting board.

To serve, carefully portion with a sharp knife, and serve each slice on a medium sized plate with a small green salad.

WARM POTATO PANCAKE WITH SMOKED SALMON AND CHIVE CRÈME FRAÎCHE

THIS IS AN ULTRA-LIGHT POTATO PANCAKE RECIPE WHICH IS VERY VERSATILE. ADD SOME SWEETCORN, SAUTÉED LEEKS OR FRESH TRUFFLE TO THE BATTER IF YOU LIKE. IT COULD ALSO BE AN ACCOMPANIMENT TO A MAIN COURSE OR SERVED SIMPLY ON ITS OWN WITH BUTTER.

SERVES 8

6 large slices of smoked salmon, about 350g (12oz)

250g (9oz) floury potatoes, peeled and quartered

2 tablespoons plain flour

2 eggs, separated

4 tablespoons double cream

2 tablespoons unsalted butter

250ml (8 fl oz) crème fraîche

1 bunch fresh chives, finely snipped

½ lemon

salt and freshly ground white pepper

Pre-heat the oven to Gas Mark 4/180°C/350°F.

Prepare the smoked salmon by trimming off any dark pieces. Carefully roll up each slice so that it makes a neat bundle or rosette.

Place the potatoes in a pan, cover with salted water, bring to the boil then simmer for 20–30 minutes until tender. Drain them well and then mash the potatoes, making sure there are no lumps. Gently stir in the flour and then the egg yolks. Beat in just enough of the cream, a spoonful at a time, until you have a thick batter, the consistency of a medium porridge. Do not add all 4 tablespoons of the cream if the batter is thin enough. This will depend on the amount of water the potatoes absorbed during cooking. Whisk the egg whites until they are light and frothy then fold into the batter.

Heat a small cast iron oven-proof frying-pan over a gentle heat until it is very hot. Add the butter, let it foam and add a large spoonful or two of the batter. It will spread a little and find its own thickness. Cook for 3–4 minutes over a gentle heat until the entire pancake seems to be setting. Turn it over and cook for a further 2 minutes. Place it in the warmed oven, still in the frying-pan, for 1–2 minutes; this will help to set the entire pancake. This is not absolutely necessary but it will help to ensure that it is properly cooked. Drain slightly on kitchen paper and continue to cook the rest of the pancakes.

To make the chive *crème fraîche*, mix the *crème fraîche* with the chives, a few drops of lemon juice and some salt and pepper to taste.

To serve, place a pancake on each plate. Top with a rosette of smoked salmon and a large dollop of *crème fraîche*.

ULSTER FRY

WHAT MAKES AN ULSTER FRY DIFFERENT OR BETTER THAN ANY OTHER FRY UP? IT'S THE FRIED
SODA AND POTATO BREAD, OF COURSE. IF THIS WASN'T SUCH A CHOLESTEROL-PACKED DISH, PAUL
COULD EAT IT EVERY DAY!

SERVES 4

2 rashers streaky bacon

2 tablespoons vegetable oil

4 rashers back bacon

1 ripe tomato, halved

salt and freshly ground white
pepper

1 Soda Farl (see p. 152)

2 Potato Bread scones (see
p. 143)

1 teaspoon unsalted butter

2–4 free-range eggs

2 tablespoons water

Fry the streaky bacon in a large frying-pan with the vegetable oil. When almost cooked, add the back bacon and the tomato halves, seasoned with salt and pepper. Cook until the streaky rashers are crispy, the back bacon is cooked but not dried out and the tomatoes are just beginning to soften. Transfer them all to a warm oven, reserving the fat in the pan.

Cut the soda bread farl in half lengthways and then each side in half again, ending up with 4 pieces. Cut the potato bread in 2. Dip the pieces into the reserved fat which was left in the pan, let them soak up a little and then drain away any excess. Dry-fry the pieces of bread gently until they are starting to crisp up. Remove them from the pan and reserve in a warm oven.

To fry the eggs in a non-stick pan, allow the teaspoon of butter to melt until it is sizzling. Crack the eggs carefully into the pan, add the water and a little salt and cover the pan. Allow them to cook slowly for about 2 minutes or until they are done to your taste.

Serve at once on to warm plates dividing up the bacon, bread, tomato and eggs.

POTATO BREAD

THIS SIMPLE GRIDDLE BREAD IS SO MOIST AND FLAVOURSOME THAT IT DOESN'T REALLY NEED
THE REST OF THE ULSTER FRY. THIS IS PAUL'S MOTHER'S VERSION.

SERVES 4

750g (1½lb) potatoes, freshly
boiled and still hot

65g (2½oz) plain flour

a pinch of salt

30–60g (1–2 oz) unsalted
butter, melted

Pre-heat a griddle or heavy-based frying-pan to hot.

Have the potatoes peeled, boiled, drained and mashed to very smooth. While the potatoes are still hot, sprinkle on the flour and salt and mix together. Add the melted butter and knead briefly; not too much or the dough will toughen.

On a floured work surface, roll out into a big circle about 1cm (½in) thick. Cut into quarters and cook on a hot griddle until brown. This will take about 3 minutes. Turn over and cook out the other side for about 2 minutes.

These potato breads are best eaten fresh but will keep quite well and can be re-heated the following day.

CREAMY POTATO GRATIN

JEANNE'S SISTER-IN-LAW SAYS THAT SHE SHOULD GIVE UP COOKING ALL OTHER
POTATO RECIPES AND JUST USE THIS ONE.

SERVES 4

500g (1lb 2oz) potatoes,
peeled and thinly sliced

salt and freshly ground white
pepper

a pinch of freshly grated
nutmeg

1 garlic clove, finely chopped

1.2 litres (2 pints) whipping
cream

Pre-heat the oven to Gas Mark 3/160°C/325°F.

Put the sliced potatoes into a large bowl and season with salt and pepper and a pinch of nutmeg. Rub the seasonings into the potatoes with your hands to ensure that they are evenly distributed. Mix the garlic with the cream then mix well with the rest of the ingredients in the bowl.

Tip the mixture into a heavy ceramic gratin dish and pat them down. Cover with greaseproof paper and cook in the pre-heated oven for 1 hour.

If desired, you can remove the greaseproof paper and brown the top under a hot grill for about 2 minutes until nice and golden brown.

Two Ways with New Potatoes

Paul grew up in Co. Down which is famous for its Comber potatoes. Each year we are amazed by the delicacy of new potatoes. When freshly dug, their fine skin can be eased off with thumb and forefinger, and the flavour is sweet and pure. After a day the skin starts to toughen, and it seems to Paul that they loose a little of their finesse. So treat them as any delicate vegetable, buy them as close to source and as fresh as possible.

General Preparation

Wash and lightly scrub the potatoes in cold water. Place in a large saucepan, and cover with cold water, with 1 tablespoon of salt. Bring to the boil, and then simmer for about 10–15 minutes, or until the tip of a knife pierces each potato easily. Drain and cover until ready to use.

New Potatoes with Peas and Ham

serves 4

125g (4$\frac{1}{2}$oz) peas, freshly
shelled

4 tablespoons water

pinch of salt

50g (2oz) fresh unsalted
butter

75g (3oz) cooked ham, cut
into $\frac{1}{2}$ cm ($\frac{1}{4}$ in) dice

250g (9oz) hot new potatoes,
freshly cooked

1 tablespoon fresh mint or
parsley, chopped

Put the peas, water, salt and 1 tablespoon of butter into a medium saucepan. Cover and cook vigorously for 3 minutes or until the peas are just cooked. Add the cooked ham dice, potatoes, mint (or parsley) and remaining butter. Shake the pan gently until the butter becomes creamy and saucelike. Serve at once. This is an ideal accompaniment to spring lamb.

NEW POTATOES WITH CREAMED HORSERADISH AND SMOKED SALMON

SERVES 4 (AS A STARTER)

250g (9oz) new potatoes, cooked, and sliced while still warm

salt and freshly ground white pepper

1 tablespoon fresh chives, snipped

1 tablespoon fresh dill, roughly chopped

2 tablespoons of prepared horseradish

120g (4½ oz) smoked salmon, cut into julienne strips

Lightly season the sliced potatoes with some salt and pepper. Toss gently with the herbs and horseradish cream while still warm. Top with strips of smoked salmon, and serve.

BAKED POTATO SKINS WITH AVOCADO, CHEDDAR AND SALSA

AN AGELESS SNACK, GREAT FOR FOOTBALL MATCHES ON TV, OR SITTING AROUND A FIRE, AN 'AFTER THE PUB' NIBBLE, OR EVEN A COCKTAIL PARTY. KIDS LOVE IT TOO!

SERVES 4

2 litres (3½ pints) vegetable oil

6 large baking potatoes

salt

2 avocadoes, diced

4 spring onions, thinly sliced

250g (9oz) Cheddar, grated

1 jar Mexican-style salsa

1 bunch chopped fresh coriander

freshly ground black pepper

Pre-heat the vegetable oil in a large pan or a deep-fat fryer to 180°C/350°F when a cube of bread will brown in 1 minute. Pre-heat the oven to Gas Mark 3/160°C/325°F.

Bake the potatoes in the pre-heated oven for 1 hour. (Or you can cook them in a microwave oven at full power for about 20 minutes.)

When they are cooked, cut each in half lengthways and scoop out most of the middle to form boat-like shapes. Reserve the scooped out potato for another use. Cut each half in half again to have quarters lengthways.

Increase the oven temperature to Gas Mark 6/200°C/400°F.

Deep-fry the skins for about 4 minutes or until nice and crisp. Drain on kitchen paper and seaon with salt. Arrange open side up on a baking sheet. Top with chopped avocado, spring onions and cheese and bake in the pre-heated oven for 5 minutes or until the cheese is nicely melted and beginning to brown. Top with spoonfuls of salsa, freshly ground pepper and sprinkle with lots of freshly chopped coriander.

CHAPTER

14

THE WATERMILL

WATERMILLS HAVE BEEN a part of the Irish land-scape since medieval times. The abundant source of water that her climate guarantees accounts for a large number of fast-flowing streams throughout the countryside, and to harness this energy was only logical. It wasn't until the end of the nineteenth century, with the introduction of the steam engine, that the reliance on these mills for food production (and industrial use as well) went into slow decline. Oats were probably the commonest grain in days gone by, but barley and rye as well as wheat were also grown and milled. Today, there are relatively few mills actually in pro-duction. Those which are seem to be aimed mostly at the healthy, alternative food market, producing organic wheat and its products. Hopefully, however, as more and more people raise their standards, through food awareness and growing knowledge and understanding that you really are what you eat, these type of wholesome food producers will be more and more in demand. Con-gratulations to those determined enough to be pioneers of the movement towards better quality food products.

What can be as satisfying and as nourishing as a whole-some loaf of bread? In some form or another, it has been the mainstay of Western man's diet for centuries. This holds true in Ireland as well. Having said that, however, the staple breads of this island have two variations which set them apart. Firstly, it was only in the last few decades that yeast has been widespread as a leavening agent. Traditionally, buttermilk and later bicarbonate of soda were used. Secondly, the traditional Irish hearth had no oven, consequently all the breads made were either cooked on a griddle set above the fire or in a type of enclosed pot or Dutch oven that could be set amongst the coals. As a result, Ireland boasts a wealth of various soda breads, scones, griddle cakes and the like – all of which can quite easily be reproduced in a heavy frying-pan on the top of a modern stove. Don't be afraid of them, it's simply another technique for you to master.

One area every Irish kitchen seems to rate highly, is in its baking. Making cakes, biscuits and teabreads was and is a tradition in which the Irish housewife tends to pride herself. Nowadays, with home baking seeming to be in decline for the most part elsewhere, it's absolutely delightful to walk into a home and smell those enticing aromas. Paul's mother and aunt are great examples of this lingering tradition. We have learned so much over the years from them both. It is just a shame that everyone can't have a grandma, aunt or mother to pass on all these precious, gratifying secrets.

CRUSTY FARMHOUSE WHITE BREAD

(V)

THERE'S NOTHING LIKE THE HEADY AROMA OF BREAD, FRESH FROM THE OVEN. IT IS A BALANCED HARMONY OF SIMPLE INGREDIENTS AND IT TRULY IS WORTH EVERY SHRED OF EFFORT IT IS GIVEN. YOU CAN BAKE THE LOAVES IN TINS OR SHAPE THEM HOWEVER YOU CHOOSE.

MAKES 2 × 450G (1LB) LOAVES

25g (1oz) fresh yeast or 15g ($\frac{1}{2}$oz) dried yeast

900ml (1$\frac{1}{2}$ pints) warm water (approximately 40°C/104°F)

1kg (2lb 4oz) strong plain flour

25g (1oz) salt

50g (2oz) unsalted butter

Blend the yeast with one-third of the water and leave for 10 minutes until it becomes frothy and foamy. This is called 'proofing the yeast'.

Put the flour, salt and butter into a mixer fitted with a dough hook. Process on medium speed and add all the yeast liquid and the remaining water together. Beat on medium speed until the dough has come together, looks rather shiny and has a nice elasticity. It should not be sticky. Alternatively, blend the ingredients and knead by hand; this will take considerably longer.

Turn out the dough into a large, clean, oiled bowl and cover with oiled cling film. Leave to rise at room temperature for 1$\frac{1}{2}$–2 hours until it has doubled in size.

If you prefer a more developed flavour and have the time, punch down the dough, again form into a ball and return the dough to the bowl to rise a second time.

This time need not be quite so long: 1–1$\frac{1}{2}$ hours should suffice.

Grease 2 × 450g (1lb) loaf tins or 2 baking sheets. To form the loaves to be baked in the bread tins, you don't really have to punch down the dough, the shaping of the loaf will usually dispel the bubbles enough and react-ivate the gluten and yeast. Firstly, divide the dough in half. Flatten the first piece using the heel of your hand then fold the dough over on itself. Basically, you are rolling a long cylinder shape. Roll it back and forth a little to smooth the surface. When it is placed into the tin the fold should be at the bottom. Repeat with the other piece. Cover the tins with oiled cling film and leave to rise again until doubled in size.

If you are forming round or oval loaves to be baked on a flat baking sheet, you may want to punch down the dough a little more. Simply lift and slap the dough down a few times on your work surface, folding it over on itself in between. With your hands, working the dough in a counter-clockwise rotary action, roll one half of the dough until the folds are tucked underneath and the whole surface is smooth and taut. Place on to the prepared baking tray. Repeat with the other half. Cover the loaves with oiled cling film and leave to rise until doubled in size.

Pre-heat the oven to Gas Mark 6/200°C/400°F.

Just before putting the loaves into the pre-heated oven you can slash the surface firmly with a very sharp knife. Besides being decorative, this makes for more crust, which appeals to some individuals. Spray the loaves generously with a mister before putting them into the oven, this improves the crust by making it more crisp.

Bake in the pre-heated oven for 15 minutes then reduce the oven temperature to Gas Mark 4/180°C/350°F for a further 30 minutes to ensure that the crust does not brown too much. The loaves are cooked when you tap the bottom and get a good hollow sound. Cool on a wire rack and do not wrap until completely cool.

WHEATEN BREAD

FOR THOSE WHO HAVE NEITHER THE TIME NOR THE INCLINATION TO MAKE THE PRECEDING YEAST BREAD, THIS WHEATEN LOAF IS SIMPLICITY ITSELF. THROW THE INGREDIENTS TOGETHER, BAKE IT OFF AND VOILÀ—A VERY QUICK, HASSLE-FREE AND TASTY LOAF.

MAKES 1 × 1 KG (2 LB) LOAF

350g ($\frac{3}{4}$lb) wholemeal flour, preferably a coarse one
150g (5oz) plain white flour
15g ($\frac{1}{2}$oz) bran
1$\frac{1}{2}$ teaspoons baking soda
pinch of salt
1 tablespoon soft brown sugar
600ml (1 pint) buttermilk

Pre-heat the oven to Gas Mark 6/200°C/400°F.

Stir all the dry ingredients together. Stir in the buttermilk to form a nice dropping consistency. Pour into a well-greased tin and bake in the pre-heated oven for about 1–1$\frac{1}{4}$ hours. Cool on a wire rack. Alternatively, if you prefer a softer crust, wrap in a lightly dampened cloth and leave to cool.

OVERLEAF

Left: *Pear and Chocolate Almond Cream Tart with Chocolate Sauce* (page 154)

Centre: *Decadent Chocolate Brownies* (page 159)

Right: *Oatmeal Muffins* (page 153)

Background: *Crusty Farmhouse White Bread* (page 148)

IRISH SODA FARLS

(V)

THESE GRIDDLE BREADS KEEP BETTER THAN OVEN-BAKED SODA BREAD. SPLIT IN TWO AND SERVED WITH PLENTY OF BUTTER AND JAM, THEY ARE THE PERFECT MATCH FOR A MORNING CUP OF TEA.

SERVES 4

450g (1lb) plain flour
$\frac{3}{4}$ teaspoon bicarbonate of soda
a pinch of salt
a pinch of sugar
1 teaspoon vegetable oil
450–550ml (15–18 fl oz)
buttermilk

Pre-heat a griddle or heavy frying-pan to hot but not smoking.

Sift together all the dry ingredients into a bowl and make a well in the centre. Pour in the oil and the lesser quantity of buttermilk and mix gently and quickly together. The resulting dough should be soft and fairly slack; add more buttermilk if necessary.

Turn out on to a work surface and knead lightly for 1 minute. Work into a large flat cake, about 1–1.5cm ($\frac{1}{2}$–$\frac{3}{4}$ in) thick, any thicker and it may not cook through properly. Cut a deep cross through the surface to make 4 triangular farls.

The griddle or pan should be hot enough to brown a little flour when sprinkled on, the heat should be somewhere between moderate to hot. If it is, place the farls on to the griddle and cook for about 6–10 minutes each side. Obviously, if the crust starts to burn, the griddle or pan is too hot.

To serve, split each farl in half and spread thickly with butter. When a day or two old, the farls can be split and toasted and will be equally delicious.

OATMEAL MUFFINS

(V)

FOR THOSE WHO CANNOT FACE UP TO A STEAMING BOWL OF PORRIDGE EVERY MORNING,
THESE MUFFINS OFFER A QUICK, EASY AND JUST AS HEALTHY, ALTERNATIVE. THEY COULD BE MADE
SWEETER, IF DESIRED, BUT WHEN MADE AS FOLLOWS, THERE IS A WHOLESOME, NUTRITIOUS FEELING
TO THEM. USE GOOD, OLD-FASHIONED OATS, NOT THE INSTANT VARIETIES.
THESE MUFFINS COULD BE FILLED WITH ANY VARIETY OF FRUIT, DRIED FRUIT AND FLAVOURINGS.
JUST REMEMBER TO BE GENEROUS WITH WHICHEVER YOU CHOSE. THE MOST IMPORTANT FACTOR
FOR GREAT MUFFINS IS TO AVOID OVERMIXING — THAT WOULD RESULT IN A TOUGH, CHEWY MUFFIN.

MAKES 24 MUFFINS

225g (8oz) rolled oats

750ml (1¼ pints) buttermilk

300g (11oz) plain flour

*1½ teaspoons bicarbonate of
soda*

1½ teaspoons salt

200g (7oz) soft brown sugar

*grated rind and juice of 1
lemon*

*3 tablespoons unsalted butter,
melted*

3 eggs

*100g (4oz) dates, chopped
and tossed in just enough
flour to coat*

*150g (5oz) finely chopped
apple, tossed in the lemon
juice*

Leave the oats to soak in the buttermilk overnight or for at least a few hours. Pre-heat the oven to Gas Mark 4/ 180°C/350°F. Line 24 muffin trays with paper muffin cases.

Sift the dry ingredients together in a large bowl. Combine the soft brown sugar and the lemon rind and add it to the bowl. By hand mix in the oats mixture. Stir in the melted butter and eggs until just combined. Finally, fold in the dates and apples, having tossed them in lemon juice. Note that the apples must be chopped quite finely to ensure that they will cook completely in the short

cooking time of the muffins. Fill the prepared muffin cases generously until about two-thirds full. Bake in the pre-heated oven for about 17–20 minutes. Muffin tins can vary in the size of their moulds so bear this in mind. Cool on wire racks and eat immediately or keep in an airtight container if desired.

PEAR AND CHOCOLATE ALMOND CREAM TART WITH CHOCOLATE SAUCE

IT IS AMAZING TO ME HOW WELL PEARS AND CHOCOLATE GO TOGETHER; THEY REALLY MAKE A TASTY COMBINATION. THIS ALMOND CREAM CAN BE MADE WITHOUT CHOCOLATE; IT THEN MARRIES WELL WITH APRICOTS, PEACHES OR CHERRIES.

SERVES 4–6

FOR THE TART

250g (9oz) Sweet Shortcrust Pastry (see p. 184)

1 egg yolk, lightly beaten

$\frac{1}{2}$ quantity Chocolate Almond Cream (see p. 185), removed from the fridge to soften

4–6 poached pears, drained and sliced into fans

Poaching Syrup (see p. 187)

25g (1oz) blanched almonds, flaked or chopped

FOR THE CHOCOLATE SAUCE

350g (12oz) plain chocolate

300ml ($\frac{1}{2}$ pint) milk or single cream, or use half of each

75g (3oz) caster sugar

50g (2oz) unsalted butter

FOR THE GLAZE

3 tablespoons apricot jam

3 tablespoons Sugar Syrup (see p. 187) or Poaching Liquid

Grease a 23–25cm (9–10in) fluted flan tin.

Roll out the pastry to about 5mm ($\frac{1}{4}$in) thick and use to line the prepared tin. Leave to rest in the fridge for at least 30 minutes.

Pre-heat the oven to Gas Mark 4/180°C/350°F. Cover the pastry with greaseproof paper and line with baking beans. Blind bake the tart in the pre-heated oven for about 10 minutes until it is golden. Brush the whole of the inside lightly with egg yolk. This helps to seal the pastry during cooking.

Reduce the oven temperature to Gas Mark 3/160°C/325°F.

With a piping bag without a nozzle (or a palette knife), evenly distribute the chocolate almond cream over the base of the tart to no more than 2cm ($\frac{3}{4}$in) thick. Arrange the pear fans decoratively on top of the chocolate almond cream, pressing them gently into the cream. Sprinkle flaked or chopped almonds generously over the top and place the tart on a baking sheet. Bake in the pre-heated oven for about 30–45 minutes. It is important that the chocolate almond cream is completely cooked. A skewer inserted in the middle should come out clean. Remove from the oven and leave to cool.

A light glaze will improve the tart's appearance substantially. To do this, melt a few tablespoons of apricot jam with an equal amount of sugar syrup (or poaching liquid from the pears). When it has come to the boil, use a pastry brush and lightly coat the top of the tart. The shiny appearance will not interfere with the flavour of the tart.

To make the sauce, melt the chocolate very gently in a bain-marie or in a bowl over a pan of gently simmering water. Set aside.

Place the remaining sauce ingredients together in a pan and bring to the boil. Remove from the heat and leave to cool down to just warm. If added to the chocolate while still hot, this would scald the chocolate and give a burnt, acrid flavour to the sauce. Whisk the chocolate into the milk mixture until smooth and well combined. This sauce keeps very well in the fridge and just needs to be taken out and warmed gently when needed.

Serve wedges of tart with the warm chocolate sauce.

POACHED PEARS WITH LIME SABAYON

A SIMPLE YET PLEASING DESSERT. BE VERY GENEROUS WITH THE SABAYON, EVERYONE LOVES IT.

SERVES 4

4 pears, poached (see page 187)

125ml (4¼ fl oz) poaching syrup from the pears (see page 187)

6–8 tablespoons fresh lime juice

6 egg yolks

120g (4½ oz) caster sugar

pinch of salt

125ml (4¼ fl oz) dessert wine or champagne

TO GARNISH

sprig of fresh mint, or candied lime julienne

Halve and core each pear. With a sharp knife slice each half in a fan style and lay them in a shallow dish. Macerate in enough of the poaching syrup to cover, and lace well with 3–4 tablespoons of lime juice. Leave for 1–2 hours.

To make the sabayon, place the yolks, the sugar, and a pinch of salt into a stainless steel bowl. Whisk together gently. Add the dessert wine and the remaining poaching syrup. Whisk vigorously over barely simmering water until thick and pale, for about 10 minutes. It should leave traces in the bottom of the bowl, and also leave a good, thick ribbon when dropped back on itself. Whisk in enough lime juice to give a firm tartness.

To serve, place the pear halves in a yin-yang fashion on slightly warmed plates, and spoon generously with the sabayon. Garnish with a sprig of fresh mint, or candied lime julienne.

FRUIT LOAF BREAD AND BUTTER PUDDING

INFUSING THE CUSTARD BASE WITH FRESH ORANGE REALLY HELPS BRING OUT THE FRUIT FLAVOURS
IN THIS LOAF. WE FIND THIS INTERPRETATION FAR MORE INTERESTING THAN THE USUAL ONE.
MAKING THE LOAF IN A MIXER OR FOOD PROCESSOR IS QUICKER AND FAR EASIER THAN BY HAND.

SERVES 8

FOR THE LOAF

15g ($\frac{1}{2}$oz) fresh yeast

3 tablespoons warm milk

375g (13oz) plain flour

1 teaspoon salt

25g (1oz) sugar

4 eggs

300g (11oz) unsalted butter,
at room temperature

30g (1oz) glacé cherries,
finely chopped

30g (1oz) mixed peel, finely
chopped

65g ($2\frac{1}{2}$oz) raisins or sultanas

FOR THE PUDDING

500ml (17 fl oz) milk

500ml (17 fl oz) whipping
cream

1 teaspoon vanilla essence

$\frac{1}{2}$ orange

250g (9oz) sugar

4 eggs

6 egg yolks

Grease a 450g (1lb) loaf tin.

Dissolve yeast in the warm milk and leave in a warm place for about 10 minutes until frothy. Place the flour, salt, sugar and eggs in a mixing bowl. Add the yeast mixture and mix by hand or with a dough hook on a medium speed for about 3 minutes until the dough is coming together. Slowly, little by little, add the butter, letting the dough incorporate it each time. The dough should turn shiny, elastic and be quite soft. Finally, toss in the dried fruit. Turn into a greased bowl and cover with oiled cling film. Leave to rise for about 1 hour in a warm place until doubled in size.

Turn the dough out on to a work surface and shape to fit into the prepared loaf tin. Cover with oiled cling film and leave to rise again until doubled in size. This time it should not take as long, about 40 minutes.

Pre-heat the oven to Gas Mark 5/190°C/375°F.

Bake the loaf in the centre of the pre-heated oven for about 45 minutes. It should sound hollow when tapped on the bottom. Leave to cool on a wire rack. This loaf will freeze very well if wrapped tightly in cling film.

To make the pudding, put the milk, cream, vanilla essence and orange in a pan over a medium heat and bring to the boil. Set aside and leave to infuse for about 20 minutes.

Pre-heat the oven to Gas Mark 2/150°C/300°F.

Whisk the sugar, eggs and the yolks together until the sugar has dissolved and the mixture is light and fluffy. Strain in the hot cream and milk mixture, whisking continually. Strain again through a fine sieve. Set aside.

Slice 8 × 5mm ($\frac{1}{4}$in) thick slices of the loaf. Cut off the crusts and dry out the slices either in the oven or by toasting them lightly in a toaster.

Arrange the slices attractively in 8 ovenproof bowls

and gently pour in the pudding mixture until the bowls are nearly full. Place the bowls in a bain-marie or roasting tin that is one-third full of hot water and cover with cling film. Don't worry that the cling film will melt; the oven is not hot enough.

The cling film will prevent a crust from forming on the pudding and it will also help to distribute the heat more evenly.

Bake in the bain-marie in the pre-heated oven for about 30 minutes until the puddings are just set (the middles will still be wobbly). Take out of the oven and remove the cling film. Leave to cool in the bain-marie.

Some people prefer their pudding still warm, others prefer it slightly chilled. Serve it however you prefer.

GYPSY CREAMS

THIS IS ANOTHER ONE OF THOSE TREASURED RECIPES HANDED ON TO JEANNE FROM PAUL'S MUM AND AUNT, FROM THEIR MUM, ETC. A PERFECT ACCOMPANIMENT TO AFTERNOON TEA.

MAKES ABOUT 2 DOZEN BISCUITS

120g (4½oz) unsalted butter

120g (4½oz) vegetable shortening

100g (¼lb) caster sugar

5 teaspoons boiling water

2 teaspoons golden syrup

2 teaspoons baking soda

250g (9oz) self-raising flour

2 cups rolled oatflakes

FOR THE ICING

120g (4½oz) unsalted butter

250g (9oz) icing sugar, sifted

a drop or two of coffee essence (or instant coffee dissolved in a few drops of water)

FOR GARNISH

25 walnuts, lightly toasted

Pre-heat the oven to Gas Mark 3/160°C/325°F.

Cream together the butter, shortening and the sugar in a mixer, until light and fluffy. Meanwhile mix the boiling water with the golden syrup. Pour this into the first mixture and beat together. Sift the baking soda together with the self-raising flour, and fold into the butter mixture by hand. Then fold in the flaked oats thoroughly.

On a lightly floured surface, roll out the dough to a thickness of about 1cm (½in) and, using a cutter about 3–4cm (1¼-1½in) in diameter, cut out rounds. Place them on an ungreased baking tray, and bake for approximately 12 minutes in the pre-heated oven, until golden brown. Cool on wire racks.

To make the icing, simply cream together the butter and icing sugar in the mixer until light and fluffy. Add the coffee essence. The icing should not be either too runny, or too thick. It should be a spreadable consistency, similar to the texture of peanut butter. When cool, sandwich two biscuits together with the icing. We like to garnish the top of the gypsy cream with a little blob of the icing and the top with a piece of lightly toasted walnut.

Oatmeal and Pecan Biscuits

These tasty, chewy biscuits can accompany coffee or tea, or even lend themselves as a garnish to ice-cream. I love them as a tasty snack on their own.

MAKES 24–36 BISCUITS

225g (8oz) unsalted butter, slightly softened

175g (6oz) caster sugar

175g (6oz) soft brown sugar

2 eggs

50ml (2 fl oz) milk

1½ teaspoons vanilla essence

250g (9oz) plain flour

1 teaspoon bicarbonate of soda

½ teaspoon salt

1 teaspoon baking powder

250g (9oz) pecans, chopped

120g (4½oz) rolled oats

Pre-heat the oven to Gas Mark 4/180°C/350°F. An ungreased baking sheet should be used, otherwise the biscuits will spread too much.

Beat the butter and the sugars together until light and fluffy.

Mix together the eggs, milk and vanilla essence then, as if making mayonnaise, slowly add to the butter and sugar mixture a spoonful at a time, incorporating the liquid into the butter mixture each time before adding more.

Sift together the flour, bicarbonate of soda, salt and baking powder. Fold into the egg and butter mixture. Finally, fold in the pecans and oats. Either drop spoon-sized portions on to the prepared baking sheet or first roll the spoonfuls into round balls and then place them on the sheet. Chill the spoonfuls, or balls, for at least half an hour before baking. This allows the butter in the mixture to firm up, again to prevent over-spreading during baking. They will flatten out as they cook and produce a more consistent shape and size of biscuit.

Bake in the pre-heated oven for about 8–10 minutes, depending on the size of the biscuits. They should be golden but not too hard. The finished biscuits should remain moist and slightly chewy. Cool the biscuits on a wire rack. Store in an airtight container when completely cool.

DECADENT CHOCOLATE
BROWNIES

Ⓥ

THERE'S REALLY ABSOLUTELY NOTHING IRISH ABOUT THIS RICH FUDGY BROWNIE BUT
WE'VE YET TO MEET AN IRISHMAN WHO DOESN'T FALL FOR IT. BESIDES, EVERY COOKERY BOOK
SHOULD CONTAIN AT LEAST ONE KILLER CHOCOLATE DESSERT RECIPE.

SERVES 8

90g (3½oz) plain flour

150g (5oz) icing sugar

20g (¾oz) cocoa

150g (5oz) plain chocolate

90g (3½oz) unsalted butter, melted

2 tablespoons golden syrup

2 eggs

1½ teaspoons vanilla essence

40g (1½oz) hazelnuts, roasted, skinned and chopped

Pre-heat the oven to Gas Mark 4/180°C/350°F. Grease a 25cm (10in) square baking tin.

Sift the dry ingredients together in a large bowl. Melt the chocolate carefully in a bain-marie or in a bowl over a pan of gently simmering water. Add the butter and the golden syrup and stir until blended. Leave to cool to lukewarm, then stir in the eggs and vanilla essence. Fold in the dry ingredients and stir rather quickly until smooth. Fold in the nuts. Pour the mixture into the tin. Bake in the pre-heated oven for 30–45 minutes. The top and edges will be crusty. The inside will be slightly gooey but not runny. Remove from the oven and leave to cool in the tin.

Cut into individual-size squares and serve while still warm with a dollop of whipped cream or, even better, vanilla ice-cream. This brownie keeps for a couple of days if wrapped completely in cling film.

CHAPTER

15

THE ORCHARD

IT IS COUNTY Armagh which carries the name 'the orchard of Ireland', and in fact it wasn't that long ago that every farmhouse had its own orchard of some size, shape or description. The persistent rain — such an integral part of the Irish climate — allows a great variety of fruit trees to thrive, and if the farmwife tended and nurtured her trees, she was rewarded with the season's bounty. Bramley and cider apples, Conference pears, Victoria plums and wild cherries all had their place, and every orchard we visited seemed to have a little corner or border reserved for the obliging bushes of raspberries, currants and gooseberries.

To a chef, especially a pastry chef, each season's harvest has an exciting allure to tempt and tease the taste-buds. Spring brings colourful rhubarb and tangy gooseberries. Those long summer days promise sumptuous soft fruits and delicious berries. Autumn is crisp crunchy apples and moist juicy pears. With such a vast array of flavours, is it any wonder that a great heritage developed? Passed from mother to daughter, neighbour to friend, a huge repertoire of humble yet pleasing desserts grew up to enhance, to emphasize, to satisfy: from crispy crumbles to silky fools, latticed tarts to double-crust pies,

steaming puddings to hearty cakes. From the windfalls and surplus, the traditions of jam-making and preserving ensured a stocked larder throughout the grey winter months.

Not only does the tended fruit flourish, but all sorts of berries proliferate throughout the countryside. Delicate elderberries hedge country lanes, blackberry brambles tumble over County Down drumlins, rowanberries bring bright confusion to the Wicklow hills, the moorland areas offer up bilberries and blackcurrants. It is simply a matter of putting on your wellies and the endless bounty is there, waiting to be picked and enjoyed.

WHITE CHOCOLATE AND CHERRY TRIFLE

THE ARRIVAL OF CHERRIES ALWAYS SIGNIFIES TO ME THE ARRIVAL OF SUMMER. MY HEART TAKES A BIG LEAP AT THE PROSPECT OF ALL THE SUMPTUOUS SOFT FRUITS TO FOLLOW. DO NOT BE PUT OFF THIS DESSERT THINKING IT SOUNDS COMPLEX AND TIME-CONSUMING — WITH A LITTLE ORGANIZATION, IT CAN BE VERY SIMPLE AND QUICK TO ASSEMBLE. YOU CAN USE ANY CHOCOLATE BISCUITS, STORE-BOUGHT OR OTHERWISE, AND THE CHERRIES CAN BE PREPARED DAYS IN ADVANCE AND STORED IN THE FRIDGE. FEEL FREE TO USE FRESH RASPBERRIES OR STRAWBERRIES IF YOU PREFER. WITH A LITTLE CARE, THE PRESENTATION OF THIS DESSERT IN AN ATTRACTIVE GLASS OR MOULD, LIFTS IT FROM THE REALM OF THE ORDINARY TO THE HEIGHTS OF DINNER-PARTY ELEGANCE.

SERVES 4–6

FOR THE BISCUIT

2 teaspoons vanilla essence

275g (10oz) plain chocolate, melted and cooled

6 eggs, separated

120g ($4\frac{1}{2}$oz) caster sugar

FOR POACHING THE CHERRIES

1 bottle deep red wine or port

500ml (17 fl oz) water

500g (1lb 2oz) sugar

1 slice of lemon

$\frac{1}{2}$ vanilla pod

450g (1lb) cherries, stoned

FOR THE WHITE CHOCOLATE MOUSSE

2 eggs

350g (12oz) white chocolate, melted and cooled slightly

100ml ($3\frac{1}{2}$ fl oz) Vanilla Anglaise (see p. 186)

400ml (14 fl oz) double or whipping cream, whipped to soft peaks

TO GARNISH

50g (2oz) plain chocolate

50g (2oz) white chocolate

a few mint leaves

Pre-heat the oven to Gas Mark 4/180°C/350°F. Grease and line a baking sheet with greased greaseproof paper.

To make the biscuit, add the vanilla essence to the melted chocolate then mix in the egg yolks.

Whisk the egg whites and sugar to firm, glossy peaks. Fold the egg whites into the chocolate mixture. Spread thinly and evenly on to the prepared baking sheet; it will be about 1cm ($\frac{1}{2}$in) thick.

Cook in the pre-heated oven for about 15 minutes until the mixture is firm. Place on a wire rack to cool. It will sink slightly as it cools.

Cut out pieces in suitable shapes to line the trifle glass or mould, keeping all the crumbs to use in the base.

To poach the cherries, place the wine or port in a large pan, bring to the boil and boil until only half the quantity remains. Add the remaining ingredients except the cherries and return to the boil. Place the stoned cherries into the poaching syrup and simmer gently for 10 minutes. Remove from the heat and leave to cool. The cherries will have a deeper, richer colour if they are left to sit in the syrup overnight. If covered in the syrup, they will keep in the fridge for weeks.

To make the mousse, place the eggs in a bain-marie or a bowl over a pan of hot water. Whisk over gentle heat until slightly warmer than body temperature. Remove from the heat and continue to whisk until cool. The eggs will be very light in colour and will double in volume.

Slowly add the melted white chocolate followed by the *crème anglaise* and then the softly whipped cream. This mousse will be quite soft, which is desired for this dessert. (For a firmer mousse, soften 2 leaves of gelatine or agar-agar in cold water, then dissolve them in a little of the *crème anglaise*, very gently warmed.) Place in the fridge for at least 1 hour before assembling the dessert.

Strain the cherries and return the syrup to the pan. Discard the lemon slice and vanilla pod. Boil the syrup until reduced by half to a syrupy consistency.

Put a layer of the chocolate biscuit in the bottom of the trifle glass or mould and soak with 1–2 tablespoons of the

poaching syrup. Ladle in enough white chocolate mousse to fill the glass by one-third and then add another layer of chocolate biscuit. Again, soak with the syrup and place a generous layer of cherries on top. (If the cherries are large, you may wish to halve them.) Ladle in another layer of mousse and again sprinkle with cherries.

Make curls of plain and milk chocolate by shaving them off the block with a peeler. Garnish the top of the trifle with big curls of white and dark chocolate and a few mint leaves. These trifles can be made several hours in advance, but if this is not the case, do not add the garnish until you are ready to serve.

AMARETTI SABLÉ OF PEACHES WITH A CARAMEL CREAM

THE ALMOND FLAVOUR OF THESE BISCUITS MARRIES PERFECTLY WITH PEACHES, ALTHOUGH APRICOTS
WOULD BE EQUALLY AT HOME IN THIS DESSERT. BE SURE YOUR FRUIT IS RIPE AND UNBLEMISHED.

SERVES 4

4 peaches

*8 × 7.5cm (3in) round
Amaretti Sable (see opposite)*

FOR THE POACHING SYRUP

*500ml (17 fl oz) dry white
wine*

500ml (17 fl oz) water

1kg (2lb 4oz) sugar

1 slice of lemon

1 slice of orange

½ vanilla pod, split

FOR THE CARAMEL CREAM

175g (6oz) caster sugar

5 tablespoons water

*200ml (7 fl oz) whipping
cream*

125g (4½oz) Mascarpone

Blanch the peaches for 10 seconds in a large pan of boiling water and then transfer them gently into a container full of cold water. This makes it very easy to peel off the skins. Bring the poaching syrup ingredients to the boil in a large pan. Add the peaches and return to the simmer. The length of time depends on the size and degree of ripeness of the peaches, but usually 5–10 minutes will suffice. If you plunge the tip of a very sharp knife into one of the peaches and the tip passes through easily to the stone, they are ready. Remove from the heat and let the peaches cool in the syrup. (This syrup can be strained and kept in the fridge for use at another time.)

To make the caramel cream, place the sugar and water in a heavy-based pan and cook over a high heat to a medium caramel, a nice amber colour. Remove from the heat and gently stir in the cream. Return to a low heat for 1–2 minutes to ensure that all the caramel has dissolved into the cream. Strain through a sieve and leave to cool. When completely cold, slowly by hand, mix together with the Mascarpone. The result should be a smooth, thick creamy texture.

To assemble the dessert, place one of the amaretti biscuits on each plate and spread a generous helping of the caramel cream on to the biscuit. Slice the peaches into fan shapes and arrange them on top of the caramel cream. Gently lay the remaining biscuits on top. Garnish with a sprinkling of ground amaretti biscuit, if desired.

AMARETTI SABLÉ

SABLÉ – IN FRENCH LITERALLY 'SAND' – REFERS TO THE DELICATE CRUMBLY TEXTURE THAT IS INHERENT IN THESE RICH, EXQUISITE BISCUITS. PAUL ALWAYS MAKES THEM IN THE FOOD PROCESSOR. BASICALLY A VERY SHORT SHORTBREAD DUE TO THE LARGE AMOUNTS OF BOTH BUTTER AND SUGAR, I FIND THAT THE GROUND AMARETTI BISCUITS ADD A DELIGHTFUL FLAVOUR THAT MARRIES WELL WITH MANY DIFFERENT FRUITS. YOU CAN BUY AMARETTI BISCUITS IN MOST SUPERMARKETS. THEY ARE HARD MACAROONS WITH A BITTER ALMOND FLAVOUR THAT COME FROM ITALY.

MAKES 24–36 DEPENDING ON SIZE

450g (1lb) plain flour

100g (4oz) amaretti biscuits, finely ground

175g (6oz) caster sugar

400g (14oz) unsalted butter, chilled and diced

2 size 1 egg yolks

2 tablespoons whipping cream

Place all the dry ingredients into a chilled bowl or food processor bowl with the diced butter. Rub together with the fingertips or a pastry cutter or pulse until the whole mixture begins to come together in pea-size consistency. Stir the yolks and cream together. Add to the bowl and work quickly with the fingertips or pulse briefly until the mixture is just coming together into a mass.

Transfer to a cold clean work surface and work with the heel of your hand until the mixture is well blended and holds together nicely. Do not overwork. Wrap in cling film and chill for at least 1 hour.

On a lightly floured surface, work with a quarter of the mixture at a time, leaving the rest in the fridge as the mixture softens very quickly. Carefully roll out to about 9mm ($\frac{3}{8}$in) thick, dusting with flour as necess-

ary. Using a cutter the size and shape you desire, cut out biscuits and gently place on an ungreased baking sheet. Chill again at this stage for at least 30 minutes. This ensures minimum shrinkage because the mixture is allowed to 'rest'. This will also help the biscuits to cook more evenly.

Pre-heat the oven to Gas Mark 4/180°C/350°F.

Bake in the pre-heated oven for 8–10 minutes until lightly golden. Leave to cool just slightly to allow the biscuits to harden a little then gently slide on to a wire rack to cool completely. Store in an airtight container. These biscuits will keep for several days.

SPICED GINGER CAKE WITH RHUBARB COMPOTE

THIS MOIST AND TASTY CAKE COULD BE PAIRED JUST AS EASILY WITH
A PLUM COMPOTE, CHUNKY APPLE SAUCE OR EVEN FRESH RIPE PEARS.

SERVES 8–10

FOR THE CAKE

175g (6oz) unsalted butter

100g (4oz) dark brown sugar

2 tablespoons freshly grated
ginger root

4 egg yolks

250g (9oz) plain flour

1 tablespoon ground ginger

$\frac{1}{2}$ teaspoon freshly grated
nutmeg

$\frac{1}{4}$ teaspoon ground cloves

$1\frac{1}{2}$ teaspoons bicarbonate of
soda

200ml (7 fl oz) molasses

100ml ($3\frac{1}{2}$ fl oz) soured cream

8 egg whites

40g ($1\frac{1}{2}$oz) caster sugar

FOR THE RHUBARB COMPOTE

1kg (2lb 4oz) rhubarb

200g (7oz) caster sugar

juice of 1 lemon

2 tablespoons grenadine

Pre-heat the oven to Gas Mark 4/180°C/350°F. Grease a 23–25cm (9–10in) spring-release cake tin.

Cream together the butter, brown sugar and fresh ginger until they are light and fluffy. Slowly add the egg yolks, mixing continually until they are all incorporated.

Sift together all the dry ingredients. Stir together the molasses and soured cream. Fold the dry ingredients and molasses mixture, alternately into the egg yolk mixture. Whisk the egg whites and caster sugar until glossy, then fold into the cake mixture. Mix everything well or there will be streaks in the cake.

Turn the mixture into the prepared tin and bake in the pre-heated oven for about 45 minutes until the sides are pulling away from the tin and a skewer inserted into the centre comes out clean. Remove from the oven, cool for 10 minutes then unmould and leave to cool completely on a wire rack. Kept wrapped completely in cling film it

will stay fresh for 2–3 days.

Finally, make the compote. If the rhubarb stalks are large they may need to be peeled so that the compote isn't stringy. Chop the stalks into roughly 2cm ($\frac{3}{4}$in) dice and place into a large heavy-based pan with the sugar and lemon juice. Cook over a gentle heat, stirring occasionally to prevent the fruit from sticking. When the rhubarb is getting soft but not mushy, remove from the heat. Pour into a bowl to stop the cooking process.

Depending on the rhubarb, a certain amount of liquid will have been released. If there seems to be too much in comparison to the amount of fruit, drain some off. Add the grenadine and stir in gently. This turns the compote to a lovely pink colour. This compote keeps well in an airtight container in the fridge.

To assemble, cut a wedge from the cake and place on a plate. Serve a generous ladle of compote beside it. A dollop of freshly whipped cream really finishes it nicely!

BRANDY SNAPS

THIS DELICATE BISCUIT CAN BE SHAPED IN VARIOUS WAYS DEPENDING UPON THE INTENDED
USE. IT PRODUCES A CRISPY LACY-LOOKING BISCUIT WHICH CAN BE SERVED ON ITS OWN
OR AS AN ACCOMPANIMENT. IF YOU LIKE, YOU CAN FREEZE THE BATTER TO USE LATER.

MAKES ABOUT 24

120g (4½oz) unsalted butter

225g (8oz) caster sugar

120ml (4 fl oz) golden syrup

120g (4½oz) plain flour

a pinch of ground ginger
(optional)

Cream the butter and sugar together by hand or in a mixer, until they are light and fluffy.

Heat the syrup gently until just warm enough to be in a more liquid state. This allows it to mix in better with the other ingredients. Slowly add to the butter and sugar mixture. Obviously if it is too warm it will cause the butter to melt and this should be avoided. Slowly work in the flour and ginger, if using, and then place in the fridge for at least 1 hour.

Pre-heat the oven to Gas Mark 6/200°C/400°F. Grease a baking sheet.

When ready to bake, pat out spoonfuls of the batter, using damp fingers, to about 3cm (1¼in) in diameter and place on the prepared baking sheet, leaving lots of room between to allow for spreading. Don't try to cook more than a few at a time because after they are cooked and cooled slightly, they will only stay malleable for seconds.

Bake in the pre-heated oven for about 3–5 minutes until they have spread, gone lacy and turned a deep golden brown. Remove from the oven and do not touch for about 1 minute. They need this time to start to set. Using a palette knife, lift and quickly shape each biscuit as needed. The inside of a bowl gives a lovely shape to serve ice-cream scoops in. Wrap around a wooden or metal cylinder to get a 'cannoli' shape, or into a horn shape by holding one edge tightly on the end of a sharpening steel and letting the other edge fan out. If the biscuits harden before you have shaped them, just return to the oven for a few seconds and they will again soften.

These biscuits will stay crisp and fresh for a couple of days if stored in an airtight container.

BRAMLEY APPLE TART WITH A WALNUT CRUMBLE TOPPING

THE BRAMLEY IS CONSIDERED BY MANY TO BE THE WORLD'S BEST COOKING APPLE. ITS NATURAL TARTNESS, WHEN COOKED, IS THE PERFECT FOIL FOR A SUGARY TOPPING SUCH AS THIS CRUMBLE.

SERVES 4

1 quantity Sweet Shortcrust Pastry (see p. 184)

2 size 1 egg yolks for brushing pastry

FOR THE FILLING

8–10 Bramley apples, about 500g (1lb 2oz)

grated rind and juice of 1 lemon

100g (4oz) caster sugar

2 teaspoons ground cinnamon

50g (2oz) unsalted butter

FOR THE CRUMBLE

75g (3oz) granulated sugar

75g (3oz) soft brown sugar

40g (1½oz) plain flour

1 teaspoon ground cinnamon

75g (3oz) walnuts, toasted, peeled and chopped

65g (2½oz) cold butter, diced

Pre-heat the oven to Gas Mark 5/190°C/375°F. Grease a 23–25cm (9–10in) tart tin.

Line the prepared tin with the shortcrust pastry rolled to a thickness of about 3mm (⅛in). Chill for 30 minutes. Cover the pastry with greaseproof paper and fill with baking beans. Bake blind in the pre-heated oven for about 20 minutes until nice and golden. Remove the paper and beans. Brush the base and sides with egg yolk. This seals the shortcrust from the filling, thus preventing a soggy crust.

Peel, core and roughly chop the apples. Toss in the lemon juice. Sprinkle over the lemon rind, sugar and cinnamon and mix in.

Melt the butter in a large pan over a moderate heat. Add the apple mixture and cook over a moderate heat, stirring frequently so that it does not stick, until the apples turn to mush, almost all the juices have evaporated and the filling is fairly dry. You may need to add more sugar depending on your taste and how tart the apples are, but remember, the crumble topping will add lots of sweetness.

Place all the crumble ingredients together in a bowl or food processor and rub together with the fingertips or a pastry cutter or pulse until it is of pea-size consistency. Be very careful not to overprocess or the butter will start to melt and the topping will become a heavy mass. Store in the fridge until needed.

Increase the oven to Gas Mark 6/200°C/400°F.

To assemble, spoon a generous amount of filling into the base, taking care not to let it fall over the edge of the mould. Sprinkle lots of the topping over the apple filling but again, take care to avoid the edges of the tart. Bake in the pre-heated oven for about 15 minutes until the topping is cooked, looking golden and crisp. Remove from the oven and leave to cool.

Slice into wedges when just warm and serve with whipped cream or *crème fraîche*.

DEEP DISH APPLE PIE

(V)

EVERYONE LOVES APPLE PIE; IT IS ONE OF THOSE HUMBLE, COMFORTING DESSERTS
ALWAYS WELCOME, ESPECIALLY ON THOSE DARK CHILLY EVENINGS.

SERVES 4

450g (1lb) Sweet Shortcrust
Pastry (see p. 184)

1kg (2lb 4oz) Cox's Orange
Pippin or other tasty eating
apple

juice of 2 lemons

grated rind of 1 lemon

500ml (17 fl oz) soured cream

2 size 1 eggs

350g (12oz) caster sugar

1 tablespoon vanilla essence

75g (3oz) plain flour

2 size 1 egg yolks for brushing
pastry

Roll out the shortcrust to 3mm ($\frac{1}{8}$in) thick and cut into 2 rounds, one having about 25cm (10in) diameter and the other having about 28–30cm (11–12in) diameter. Chill for 30 minutes.

Peel and finely slice the apples and toss in the lemon juice. Set aside. Stir together all the other ingredients in a separate bowl until smooth and homogenous.

Grease a slope-sided pie dish and line it with the smaller round of pastry. Chill again for 30 minutes.

Pre-heat the oven to Gas Mark 4/180°C/350°F.

Brush the base of the tart with egg yolk. This helps to seal the pastry, thus preventing it from getting too soggy during baking.

Toss the apples with the soured cream filling and pile the whole mixture into the base, heaping into a generous dome. The soured cream mixture will set as it cooks, so do pour it all in as long as it does not overflow the base.

Take the second pastry round from the fridge. Brush the perimeter of the pastry base with egg yolk, and gently lay the pastry on the top, sealing the edges of the pastry together. Trim the edges so that a sealed margin of about 2cm ($\frac{3}{4}$in) is left. This margin can then be pinched into a decorative shape with thumb and forefinger. With a knife tip, slit the lid in a few places to allow the steam to escape during cooking and brush the top of the lid with egg yolk. This will turn nice and shiny golden as it bakes.

Bake in the pre-heated oven for about 45–55 minutes. The pastry should be firm and golden and the apple slices should pierce easily with a skewer. Remove from the oven and leave to cool. Serve when just warm with a big scoop of *crème fraîche*, whipped cream, or a cinnamon ice-cream.

OVERLEAF

Left: *Honey and Ginger Ice-cream with a Plum Compote* (*page 172*)

Right: *Bramley Apple Tart with a Walnut Crumble Topping* (*page 168*)

HONEY AND GINGER
ICE-CREAM WITH A PLUM COMPOTE

NOTHING BEATS A HOME-MADE ICE-CREAM. USING QUALITY INGREDIENTS ENSURES THAT.
WE ALWAYS USE AN ICE-CREAM MACHINE AS YOU CANNOT QUITE REPRODUCE THE SAME
QUALITY BY HAND. FRUIT COMPOTES PROVIDE AN EXCELLENT ACCOMPANIMENT, BUT THEY CAN
BE A DESSERT IN THEIR OWN RIGHT WITH JUST A DOLLOP OF FRESH CREAM.

SERVES 6–8

FOR THE ICE-CREAM

500ml (18 fl oz) milk

500ml (18 fl oz) whipping
cream

2 tablespoons peeled and
chopped fresh root ginger

$\frac{1}{2}$ vanilla pod

12 egg yolks

150g (5oz) caster sugar

100ml ($3\frac{1}{2}$ fl oz) clear honey

chopped candied ginger to
garnish

FOR THE PLUM COMPOTE

900g (2lb) plums, halved and
stoned

about 450g (1lb) sugar,
depending on the tartness of
the plums

$\frac{1}{2}$ vanilla pod

$\frac{1}{2}$ cinnamon stick

1 slice of orange

mint leaves to garnish

To make the ice-cream, put the milk, cream, ginger and vanilla pod in a large pan. Bring to the boil then remove from the heat and leave to infuse for 1 hour.

Whisk the egg yolks and sugar together until light and fluffy. Return the milk mixture to the boil and then, whisking continuously, pour on to the egg yolk mixture. Return the whole mixture to the pan over a low heat, and stir continuously with a wooden spoon until it thickens enough to coat the back of the spoon. If you draw your finger across it, it will hold the line on the spoon. If it does not hold the line then it is not cooked enough. Remove from the heat when the right consistency has been reached and strain through a fine conical sieve. Leave to cool, stirring continuously, then stir in the honey. Leave to cool.

Turn in to an ice-cream machine and proceed accord-ing to the manufacturer's instructions. Alternatively, pour into a freezer container and freeze until firm, whisking every 30 minutes to break up the ice crystals.

Candied ginger can either be sprinkled into the ice-cream during the final whisking or reserved as a garnish to sprinkle over it.

To make the plum compote, place all the ingredients in a large heavy-based pan and place over a low to moderate heat. Taking care that the sugar does not burn on the bottom, cook the compote for 10–20 minutes, carefully stirring occasionally, trying not to mash the plums, until they are soft. The time will depend on the size and ripeness of the plums. They should be soft but still hold their shape. Remove from the heat and leave to cool in the juices released during cooking.

There is usually a lot of liquid released. Strain this off

the plums back into a pan and boil until reduced by half to concentrate the flavour. However, if it is reduced too much, it tends to be bitter, so taste regularly to check for this. You may find that you only want to add a little of this liquid back to the plums, depending on what you are then using them for.

Meanwhile, with the tip of a sharp knife, the job of skinning the plums should now be relatively easy. These plums can be kept in halves, quarters or chopped roughly, depending on what the compote is going to be used for. The compote keeps very well in the fridge in a sealed container.

Serve the ice-cream in a brandy snap basket (see p. 167), surrounded with the plum compote. Garnish with mint leaves.

PLUM CLAFOUTIS

A DESSERT USUALLY RESERVED FOR CHERRIES, I SEE NO REASON WHY ONE CANNOT ADAPT THIS FRENCH SPECIALITY TO PLUMS, OR, FOR THAT MATTER, APRICOTS. A THINNER-SKINNED PLUM SUCH AS GREENGAGE (REINE CLAUDE) IS MORE DESIRABLE.

SERVES 4

1 tablespoon unsalted butter

450g (1lb) plums, halved and stoned

25g (1oz) pastry flour

pinch of salt

50–75g (2–3oz) caster sugar (more if plums are really tart)

3 eggs

450ml (15 fl oz) whole milk

2 egg yolks

drop or two almond essence

2 teaspoons vanilla esssence

icing sugar

Pre-heat the oven to Gas Mark 4/180°C/350°F.

Butter a shallow oven dish well with the unsalted butter. Place the plum halves fairly tightly together over the bottom of the dish. Sift together the flour, salt and the sugar. Slowly mix in the eggs by hand, followed by the milk. Do not mix excessively, as this type of batter can be toughened by too much handling. Beat in the yolks and essences, and pour the batter over the plums.

Bake in the oven for about 40 minutes, until the batter has risen and is golden brown. Remove from the oven and dust liberally with icing sugar.

APPLE TARTE TATIN WITH BRAMLEY APPLE SORBET

TARTE TATIN, ONE OF THOSE GREAT FRENCH CLASSICS THAT NEVER SEEMS TO DATE OR GO OUT OF STYLE. WHAT ELSE NEEDS TO BE SAID? WE ALWAYS USE A FOOD PROCESSOR TO MAKE SORBETS AS YOU GET THE BEST RESULTS.

SERVES 6

FOR THE TART

about 250g (9oz) Puff Pastry (see p. 182–3)

12–16 crunchy eating apples (Granny Smith, Cox, etc.)

juice of 2 lemons

165g (5½oz) unsalted butter, at room temperature

175–215g (6–7½oz) caster sugar, less for a sweeter apple, more for the tarter-tasting apple

FOR THE BRAMLEY APPLE SORBET

500ml (17 fl oz) dry cider

400g (14oz) caster sugar

grated rind and juice of 1 lemon

500g (1lb 2oz) Bramley apples, peeled and chopped

Pre-heat the oven to Gas Mark 6/200°C/400°F.

Roll out the puff into a round, about 3mm (⅛in) thick; no thicker than 5mm (¼in) or it will not cook properly. Chill this round in the fridge for at least 30 minutes.

Meanwhile, peel, core and halve the apples, tossing generously in the lemon juice.

Take a medium heavy-based, ovenproof frying-pan or medium-sized, ovenproof, low-sided pan and with a spatula, spread the butter evenly all over the base. Sprinkle on all the sugar, again distributing evenly. Starting at the perimeter, arrange the apple halves on their side, in a pinwheel fashion, filling the middle after a full circle of halves is in place. These need to be quite tightly packed or they will fall over in the cooking process.

Place the pan over a high heat and watching that no part of the butter/sugar starts to burn or blacken, cook until it has all turned golden and caramel. At this point, you may want to squeeze in one more apple half to ensure that they all stay upright. This part of the cooking process will take about 15 minutes, depending on the heat.

Carefully lay the chilled round of pastry on top of the apples, tucking in the edges and turning them down so that when it is inverted, the edges will create a rim that will hold in the apple juices and caramel. Place the pan in the pre-heated oven for about 20 minutes to cook the puff pastry as well as to finish cooking the apples.

Remove from the oven and, taking great care, loosen round the edges of the tart with a knife. Lay a plate or tray that is larger than the pan on top and quickly turn upside-down so that the tart turns out on to the plate. With a palette knife, pat any apples which have become loosened back into place and leave to cool. All the juices will be reabsorbed and the caramel will set slightly because of the pectin released from the apples.

To make the Bramley apple sorbet, put the cider, sugar, lemon rind and juice into a large pan. Place the peeled, chopped Bramleys into the liquid and simmer gently, stirring occasionally, until the apples are completely cooked and mushy. Be careful that the sugar all dissolves and doesn't catch on the bottom of the pan.

Rub the mixture through a conical sieve and leave to cool. Taste again to adjust the flavouring as this can vary so much depending on the apples. It might need a little more sugar, lemon juice or even cider. You are aiming for a slightly tart, tangy taste, not too sweet, to balance the richness of the *tarte tatin*.

Turn into an ice-cream machine and proceed according to the manufacturer's instructions or spoon into a freezer container and freeze until firm, whisking every 30 minutes to break up the ice crystals.

This sorbet can, of course, be served on its own or as an accompaniment.

To assemble the dessert, cut the *tarte tatin* into wedges and present on slightly warmed plates. Place a spoonful of sorbet at the side. (This dessert does not keep well, but not to worry because there is rarely any left).

CHAPTER

16

BASIC RECIPES

MOST OF THE RECIPES listed here are ones that are referred to several times in this book, but this is by no means a complete guide to basic recipes. We would, however, encourage any serious cook to familiarize themselves totally with them. Serious cooks should compile their own guide, from stocks and sauces through to pastas, pastries and so on. It is only through a complete understanding of the basics that a cook can become free of the need for recipes. Just as professional musicians, for example, have a strong foundation of classical techniques behind them, so a knowledge of basic methods must become ingrained in a cook. With this knowledge and understanding one has the ability to foresee possible disasters or to correct and rescue any accidents, but, more importantly, one can then move on to invent sparklingly new and original dishes.

VINAIGRETTE DRESSING

(V)

THERE ARE ENDLESS VARIATIONS WHICH COME UNDER THE DEFINITION 'VINAIGRETTE'.
BASICALLY, A LOT OF WHAT GOES INTO THE DRESSING DEPENDS UPON PERSONAL TASTE
AND WHAT THE VINAIGRETTE IS GOING TO DRESS. A GOOD RATIO TO WORK FROM IS ONE
PART VINEGAR TO FOUR OR FIVE PARTS OIL. FOR THOSE WITH FOOD ALLERGIES, A GOOD
SUBSTITUTE FOR THE VINEGAR IS LEMON JUICE.

MAKES ABOUT 250ML (8 FL OZ)

$\frac{1}{2}$ teaspoon salt

$\frac{1}{2}$ teaspoon freshly ground
black pepper

2 teaspoons Dijon mustard

2–4 tablespoons white wine
vinegar

230ml ($7\frac{1}{2}$ fl oz) olive or
vegetable oil

Dissolve the salt, pepper and mustard in the wine vinegar in a bowl. Whisk in the oil, slowly at first to allow it to be incorporated. Taste to adjust seasoning as needed. This can easily be made in a blender. Simply place all the ingredients in together and blend.

Keep all vinaigrettes in a fridge if they are not being used immediately otherwise they can develop a rancid taste to them.

MAYONNAISE

(V)

THIS IS A CLASSIC RECIPE THAT YOU CAN VARY BY THE ADDITION OF YOUR
FAVOURITE HERBS, SUCH AS BASIL OR PARSLEY.

SERVES 4

1 tablespoon Dijon mustard

salt and freshly ground white
pepper

1 tablespoon white wine
vinegar

3 egg yolks

500ml (17 fl oz) vegetable oil
or light olive oil

Whisk the mustard, salt, pepper and vinegar in a bowl until the salt has dissolved. Add the egg yolks and whisk in the oil, very slowly at first, literally drop by drop. As the mayonnaise starts to build up, you can add the oil slightly faster but always be sure to incorporate each addition fully before adding more. Continue until you have blended in all the oil and the mayonnaise is thick and creamy.

Brown Chicken Stock

Brown chicken stock is one of those invaluable items, to both the professional and the domestic chef. For convenience, make it in large batches. It can be boiled down to concentrate the flavours, and then frozen so it is always on hand.

MAKES ABOUT 3 LITRES $(5\frac{1}{4}$ PINTS)

3kg (7lb) chicken bones, wings and legs

500g (1lb 2oz) onions, chopped

500g (1lb 2oz) carrots, chopped

200g (7oz) celery, chopped

1 garlic head

100g (4oz) tomato purée

1 bouquet garni

Pre-heat the oven to Gas Mark 6/200°C/400°F.

Chop the chicken bones with a heavy knife. Roast them in a roasting tin in the pre-heated oven for about 30 minutes or until nicely brown. Add the vegetables and roast for another 10 minutes.

Transfer the bones and vegetables to a large pan and fill with cold water. Bring to the boil and skim off any fat and scum. Add the tomato purée and bouquet garni. Cover and simmer for 2 hours, skimming frequently. Strain through a fine sieve.

If you want a stronger, thicker stock, reduce the stock by boiling, or thicken with a little of your favourite gravy thickener.

Store in an airtight container in the fridge or in plastic bags in the freezer.

GOURMET PIZZA DOUGH

THIS EGG-ENRICHED DOUGH IS LIGHTER THAN THE TRADITIONAL PIZZA DOUGH SO IT MAKES
A GREAT STARTER OR SNACK. IF YOU HAVE A MIXER OR FOOD PROCESSOR YOU CAN TAKE SOME
OF THE HARD WORK OUT OF THE KNEADING PROCESS.

MAKES 6 × 18CM (7IN) ROUNDS

15g (½oz) fresh yeast or 8g
(¼oz) dried yeast

120ml (4 fl oz) warm water

350g (12oz) plain flour

a pinch of salt

2 eggs, lightly beaten

50g (2oz) butter, diced, and at
room temperature

Dissolve the yeast in the warm water and leave in a warm place for about 10 minutes until frothy.

Place flour and salt in a bowl. Add the frothy yeast mixture, the eggs and butter and mix until ingredients form a dough. Knead the dough until it is shiny, elastic and smooth. Place in a greased bowl, cover with oiled cling film and leave to rise in a warm place for about 2 hours until doubled in size.

Grease 3 baking sheets.

Lightly flour the work surface and tip out the dough. Divide into 6 portions. With a rolling pin, work each piece one at a time to a diameter of 18–20cm (7–8in); the dough will be about 5mm (¼in) thick. With your fingertips, neatly fold the edges up all the way around to give a nice rim to the dough. Place on the prepared baking sheet, and finish the other pieces in the same way. Cover with oiled cling film and again leave to rise; this time it will only take about 30 minutes.

Pre-heat the oven to Gas Mark 6–7/200–220°C/400–425°F.

Bake in the pre-heated oven for about 10 minutes until light and golden brown. Remove from the oven and cool on a wire rack.

These can be used immediately to make individual-sized gourmet pizzas or wrapped completely in cling film and placed in the fridge, or alternatively frozen until needed.

PASTA DOUGH

MAKING PASTA A SIMPLE, YET SATISFYING PROCEDURE. THE DOUGH CAN BE FROZEN UNTIL IT IS NEEDED, SO MAKE IT UP IN BIG BATCHES. DO EXPERIMENT BY ADDING HERBS OR SPICES TO THE DOUGH, THEY ADD A WHOLE NEW RANGE OF FLAVOURS. ONCE YOU'VE TRIED FRESH PASTA, YOU'LL BE HOOKED!

SERVES 6 AS A STARTER
OR 4 AS A MAIN COURSE

250–300g (9–11oz) strong plain flour (or extra fine semolina flour, or use half of each)

3 eggs

a pinch of salt

1 tablespoon oil

Mound the flour in a big pile in the centre of a work surface. Make a well in the middle and place the eggs, salt and oil into the well. Gradually, using one hand, incorporate the flour from the edges into the liquid, stirring and mixing until it all becomes one stiff dough.

Knead this dough for approximately 5–10 minutes until it is shiny, smooth and elastic. If it is too soft, add a little more flour. If it seems too dry, add a spoonful of water. These basic ingredients will react together depending on factors such as temperature and humidity, so they will vary. Once the dough is ready it must rest. Wrap it in cling film and place in the fridge for at least 30 minutes.

All this can be done on the mixer with a dough hook or even in a food processor. If made in a machine, extend the resting time to 1 hour because the flour will have been worked harder.

When it comes to rolling the dough out, the most efficient way is with one of the many hand roller type machines that are widely available. However, people have done it by hand for hundreds of years so don't feel intimidated, it is very simple to do. On a floured surface, work with a quarter of the dough at a time. With the rolling pin, work the dough out as thinly as possible, aiming for 2–4mm (less than $\frac{1}{8}$in), basically as thin as possible. Once this has been achieved it is simply a matter of cutting it into the required shape, thin strips, fat strips or whatever you choose.

If using a machine, again take just a quarter of the dough at a time and work it through the rollers, taking it thinner each time until it is the desired thinness, usually the last or second last setting.

To cook pasta uniformly and without it all sticking together, the secret is to use lots of boiling salted water. A general rule of thumb is to use 1 litre (1¾ pints) for every 100g (4oz) of pasta. Adding a tablespoon of oil to the water is also a regular recommendation. The length of cooking time will always be dependent on the type and size of the noodles but just until it is tender, but still has a slight bite, is what to aim for. Thin strips of fresh pasta will only take 3–4 minutes. Taste to see when the pasta is cooked. When the pasta is ready, drain it into a colander and use immediately.

RAVIOLI

This dough must stay slightly softer to be able to shape raviolis. To achieve this, follow the basic recipe above but add 1 egg yolk. This will give a softer, more malleable dough that will not dry out as quickly, thus allowing you time to shape the dough as well as a dough that will not crack or break once shaped.

PASTA NERA

This black dough gets its colour from the ink sac of a cuttlefish (or several sacs from several smaller squid). Again, a slight alteration to the basic dough is needed. Omit 1 whole egg from the recipe and substitute 5 tablespoons of ink from the ink sac. Be sure to add the ink by first passing it through a fine sieve. It may also be necessary to add more flour, up to 50g (2oz) at least. Mix this dough in a large bowl rather than on a work surface because it can get very messy.

SAVOURY SHORTCRUST PASTRY Ⓥ

JUST FLOUR, WATER AND BUTTER CAN PRODUCE A SATISFACTORY RESULT, BUT
I LIKE TO ENRICH THIS SHORTCRUST WITH EGGS AND CREAM. YOU CAN MAKE THIS PASTRY
BY HAND OR IN A FOOD PROCESSOR.

MAKES ABOUT 900G (2LB)

500g (1lb 2oz) plain flour

20g (¾oz) sugar

2 teaspoons salt

375g (13oz) unsalted butter, chilled and diced

2 eggs

2 tablespoons single cream

Place all the dry ingredients into a chilled bowl. Rub in the butter until the mixture forms pea-sized lumps.

Mix together the eggs and cream. Pour into the bowl and mix until the mixture comes together.

Transfer to a work surface and with the heel of your hand, work together until the mixture holds together nicely. It should now be wrapped in cling film and chilled for at least 1 hour. This firms up the butter and allows the gluten in the flour to relax.

Divide into 3 portions, wrap well and store in the fridge for up to a week or freezer for up to a month.

PUFF PASTRY

Jeanne was taught this puff pastry recipe when she worked for Albert Roux. Although she has since tried many other recipes, this is the one she keeps coming back to. Puff pastry must be one of the most rewarding pastries to make. You begin with the most basic of ingredients, yet with time and a gentle touch you end up with the most delightful results. You can make the pastry by hand or in a mixer or food processor.

MAKES JUST OVER 1KG (2¼LB)

500g (1lb 2oz) strong plain flour

75g (3oz) unsalted butter

1 tablespoon salt

1 egg yolk

220ml (7½fl oz) water

1 tablespoon white wine vinegar

600g (1lb 5oz) unsalted butter, diced

175g (6oz) strong plain flour

Place the first batch of flour together with the first batch of butter and the salt in a bowl and rub in the butter.

Stir together the yolk, water and wine vinegar and add them to the bowl. Mix the ingredients together for a good 5–10 minutes until it has all come together into a smooth, shiny dough. Wrap in cling film and place in the fridge to rest for 1 hour.

Now place the larger batch of butter with the second batch of flour into the bowl and mix to a smooth paste-like consistency. Do not mix too much or the butter will get too soft and start to melt. Remove from the bowl and tip out on to a work surface. Pat into a neat rectangle and wrap in cling film. Place in the fridge for 1 hour.

After 1 hour, remove both batches. Place the flour-based dough on a floured work surface. Roll it out to a 30cm (12in) square. Place the butter-based paste in the centre of the dough and gently, without stretching, fold all 4 sides over as if wrapping the butter-based dough like a present. The object is to enclose the butter completely so that when you start to roll them out, none of the butter can escape or leak out.

Roll the 'package' out gently but surely until you have a rectangle shape, about 20 × 46cm (8 × 18in). Brush off any excess flour and fold up the bottom third, then fold down the top third. Turn this rectangle to be lengthways on the work surface and again, roll out to the dimensions above. Fold into thirds again, the way you would a business letter, wrap in cling film and place in the fridge to chill and rest for 1 hour. This chilling and resting stage is of vital importance. The ingredients must stay cool or their properties will change, consequently your puff pastry would not end up with the right results.

After 1 hour, remove from the fridge and roll out twice more in exactly the same way as before. All this rolling is how the many layers that are in puff pastry are formed. If the puff dough is allowed to get too soft, and is forced too much, these layers would be damaged. Wrap in cling film and return to the fridge to rest again for 1 hour.

The last rolling is only one turn, not two like the previous two times. This is the classic amount of rolls and turns given to puff pastry. After it has again rested and chilled, it is ready to use. This puff freezes excellently so if you are going to go to all the effort of making it, be sure to make at least this quantity and then you will have some in the freezer, on hand, when you need it.

To roll the pastry, take one quarter of the quantity given above to roll at a time. Place on a floured work surface and with a rolling pin, gently work it out to a thickness of about 5–6mm ($\frac{1}{4}$in). This thickness, when cooked, will raise to a good 5cm (2in). Place the sheet of puff on to a baking sheet and chill for at least 20 minutes before cutting the desired shapes.

To cook the puff, place the cut pieces on to a slightly dampened baking sheet (by being damp the puff will stay in place and not slide all over when you go to egg wash it).

Usually puff pieces are egg washed on top. This is what gives it the lovely golden and shiny appearance when it is cooked. This also allows you to decorate the top if you desire, by 'drawing', gently, simple designs on to the egg wash.

Puff pastry needs to be cooked in a hot oven to puff up properly. Put it in at about Gas Mark 6/200°C/400°F. The temperature can be turned down after the first 10 minutes to about Gas Mark 4–5/180–190°C/350–375°F and then the cooking is continued for another 10–15 minutes. This ensures that the puff piece is cooked right through and that the middle won't be a soggy mass of uncooked dough.

SWEET SHORTCRUST PASTRY

THIS SHORTCRUST IS CRISP YET TENDER PASTRY, VERY WORKABLE. THE MORE SUGAR A SHORTCRUST DOUGH HAS, THE 'SHORTER' AND HARDER TO WORK WITH IT BECOMES. THE SECRET IS TO REMEMBER TO KEEP EVERYTHING COOL, BOTH INGREDIENTS AND THE BOWL. CHILL FOR 20–30 MINUTES BEFORE ROLLING AND THE SAME AGAIN AFTER ROLLING AND LINING THE TART TIN. THIS WILL GIVE THE BEST RESULTS BECAUSE THE BUTTER WILL NOT HAVE THE OPPORTUNITY TO MELT, WHICH TENDS TO MAKE THE PASTRY HEAVY AND DENSE. IT IS WORTH MAKING IN THE QUANTITY BELOW — IT IS ESPECIALLY EASY IN A FOOD PROCESSOR — AND THEN FREEZING WHAT YOU DON'T USE.

MAKES 4 × 23–25CM (9–10IN) ROUNDS

650g (1lb 7oz) plain flour
175g (6oz) caster sugar
a pinch of salt
350g (12oz) unsalted butter
3 eggs

Place all the dry ingredients in a chilled bowl. Rub in the butter until the mixture forms pea-sized lumps. Stir together the eggs then add to the bowl. Mix until it all starts to mass together.

Transfer the mixture to a work surface and, using the heel of your hand, work the mixture until it all holds together in a cohesive ball and there are no big lumps of butter unmixed. Divide into 4 even batches and wrap well in cling film. Place in the fridge. This pastry will keep in the fridge for about a week and in the freezer for about 1 month.

BAKING BLIND

Many recipes call for 'blind baking' a tart base. This is simply a pre-baking of the base. It is accomplished by lining the base with grease-proof or aluminium foil and filling with beans of some sort. This 'holds' the pastry in place until it is cooked enough to be set. The pastry is then cooked in a pre-heated oven at Gas Mark 4/180°C/350°F for about 15 minutes. Usually, after removing the paper and beans, the tart base is popped back into the oven for a minute or two to ensure that the bottom is evenly cooked to a golden brown.

CRÈME FRAÎCHE

PACKAGED CRÈME FRAÎCHE IS BECOMING WIDELY AVAILABLE IN SUPERMARKETS AND DELICATESSENS. IT IS LIGHT AND LIVELY, LESS CLOYING THAN NORMAL CREAM. IT ALSO HAS A LOWER FAT CONTENT AND IT DOESN'T CURDLE EASILY. IT IS SIMPLE TO MAKE.

MAKES 500ML (17 FL OZ)

500ml (17 fl oz) whipping or double cream

1 tablespoon buttermilk

Mix the two ingredients together. Bring to a temperature of 25–29°C (77–84°F), no hotter really than a warm room. Cover and let it stand for 8–24 hours. The longer it sits the more pronounced the tangy flavour. After 24 hours keep covered in the fridge. It will keep for 7–10 days.

CHOCOLATE ALMOND CREAM

IF PREFERRED, THIS RECIPE CAN BE MADE WITHOUT THE CHOCOLATE, ADDING RUM OR VANILLA TO FLAVOUR IT INSTEAD.

MAKES ABOUT 900G (2LB)

250g (9oz) unsalted butter

250g (9oz) caster sugar

40g (1½oz) plain flour

250g (9oz) ground almonds

4 eggs, lightly beaten

200g (7oz) plain chocolate, melted and cooled

Cream together the butter and sugar. Add the flour and then the ground almonds. Mix well. Slowly add the eggs, a little at a time, ensuring that they blend in well. Finally, pour in the melted chocolate.

This mixture, stored in a sealed container, can be kept in the fridge for several days. It is a real stand-by filling for fruit tarts and the famous classic puff pastry dessert, pithivier.

WALNUT SHORTBREAD

IF YOU USE A FOOD PROCESSOR OR MIXER, BE CAREFUL NOT TO OVER-PROCESS OR
THE BUTTER WILL START TO MELT.

MAKES 2 ROUNDS OF
12 PORTIONS OR ABOUT
24–36 5CM (2IN) ROUNDS
OR SQUARES

600g (1lb 5oz) plain flour

200g (7oz) sugar

*150g (5oz) walnuts, toasted
and ground*

*450g (1lb) unsalted butter,
chilled and diced*

Place all the ingredients in a chilled bowl and rub in the butter then mix until it all just comes together. Tip out on to a clean work surface and quickly, using the heel of your hand, make sure that all the ingredients are well mixed. Pat it into a round, wrap tightly in cling film and place in the fridge for 1 hour.

Roll the chilled piece of dough out to a thickness of no more than 1cm ($\frac{1}{2}$in). Either work it into a round shape and then cut this round into pie-type wedges, or if preferred, work into a rectangle shape and then cut into pieces as desired. Either way, this rolled piece of dough should be transferred on to a baking sheet and chilled again for at least 30 minutes.

Pre-heat the oven to Gas Mark 2/150°C/300°F.

Bake the shortbread in the pre-heated oven for 25–30 minutes. Ideally the shortbread should take little or no colour. Allow to cool and set slightly before transferring to a wire rack to finish cooling. Store in an airtight container.

VANILLA ANGLAISE (CUSTARD SAUCE)

THIS IS OUR RECIPE FOR THE STANDARD ENGLISH CUSTARD SAUCE (OR AS THE FRENCH CALL IT,
CRÈME ANGLAISE). SILKY AND SMOOTH, IT ENHANCES MOST PUDDINGS AND DESSERTS.

MAKES 500ML (17 FL OZ)

*500 ml (17 fl oz) whole milk,
(or $\frac{1}{2}$ milk, $\frac{1}{2}$ cream)*

*$\frac{1}{2}$ vanilla pod, split (or
$\frac{1}{2}$ teaspoon vanilla extract)*

6 egg yolks

120 g (4$\frac{1}{2}$ oz) castor sugar

Place the milk in a saucepan with the vanilla and bring to a boil. Set aside to let the vanilla infuse.

Whisk the yolks and sugar together in a bowl until lightened in colour, and the sugar has dissolved. Whisking continuously, slowly pour the milk into the yolk/sugar mixture and blend well.

Pour this mixture back into a clean saucepan and cook over a low heat. Stir continuously with a wooden spoon, until the mixture coats the back of the spoon, and keep on the heat until it reaches the desired consistency. Strain the mixture through a fine mesh sieve and allow to cool. Either remove the vanilla pod or leave it in the sauce which will continue to flavour it. Be sure to scrape all the seeds from inside the pod and to add them to the sauce, as these give the flavour and aroma of the vanilla pod.

This sauce can be kept in the refridgerator for up to 4 days if the milk is fresh, in a covered container.

POACHING SYRUP FOR PEARS (OR OTHER SOFT FRUITS)

THIS IS JUST A VARIATION OF THE SIMPLE SUGAR SYRUP. THE WINE AND LEMON JUICE ADD A BIT OF ACIDITY WHICH HELPS TO ACCENTUATE MOST FRUITS' FLAVOURS. ONE COULD USE A RED WINE JUST AS WELL, AND IT WOULD COLOUR THE FRUIT.

MAKES ABOUT 2 LITRES
($3\frac{1}{2}$ PINTS)

1 litre ($1\frac{3}{4}$ pints) water

1 litre ($1\frac{3}{4}$ pints) crisp white wine

1kg ($2\frac{1}{4}$lb) sugar

1 vanilla pod, split

1 clove or several black peppercorns (optional)

juice of 1 lemon

8 ripe pears

Bring all the ingredients, except the pears and half of the lemon juice, to the boil in a large pan.

Meanwhile, peel the pears and rub them with the juice of the remaining half lemon to avoid the pears discolouring. Submerge the pears in the poaching liquid and poach at a very gentle rolling boil for 10–20 minutes, depending on pear size and ripeness. When the tip of a sharp knife plunges easily through the flesh of the pears, they are done. Remove from the heat and let them cool down in the poaching liquid.

Store the pears in the fridge in the liquid, until needed. This syrup can be strained and used again and again.

SUGAR SYRUP

(V)

THIS BASE SYRUP CAN BE USED FOR SORBETS, POACHING FRUITS, SOAKING SPONGES, AND SO ON.
IT KEEPS INDEFINITELY SO IT IS ONE OF THOSE THINGS TO KEEP ON HAND AS A BASIC IN THE KITCHEN.

MAKES 500ML (17 FL OZ)

500ml (17 fl oz) water

500g (1lb 2oz) sugar

½ vanilla pod or 1 teaspoon vanilla essence

25g (1oz) glucose syrup (optional)

Place all the ingredients together in a large pan. Bring to the boil and boil for 2–3 minutes. Skim any scum that comes to the surface. This is just impurities being released from the sugar. Remove from the heat and leave to cool. Store in a sealed container in the fridge.

INDEX

Page numbers in *italic* refer to the illustrations